Larry B. Weeks
Read Monday

ALABAMA FOOTPRINTS Pioneers

A Collection of
Lost & Forgotten Stories

Read all books of the
The Alabama Footprints Series

ALABAMA FOOTPRINTS
Exploration

ALABAMA FOOTPRINTS
Settlement

ALABAMA FOOTPRINTS
Pioneers

More coming soon!

Additional stories of Alabama pioneers can be found on the websites:

www.alabamapioneers.com

www.daysgoneby.me

Follow on Facebook at:

http://www.facebook.com/alabamapioneers

http://www.facebook.com/daysgonebyme

and

Twitter

http://twitter.com/alabamapioneers

ALABAMA FOOTPRINTS

Pioneers

A Collection of
Lost & Forgotten Stories

by

Donna R. Causey

Copyright © 2015 by Alabama Pioneers
All Rights Reserved
This book, or parts thereof, may not be reproduced in any form without permission
Published by Alabama Pioneers

ISBN-13: 978-1516945641
ISBN-10: 1516945646

Kindle Edition
ASIN: B014BY5EJW

DEDICATION
This book is dedicated to all
my friends and family in Alabama

INTRODUCTION

They felt the lure of the frontier and struck out for unknown territory, bringing with them only very few implements to survive. They came from Tennessee, North Carolina, South Carolina, Georgia and many other states to settle in the newly opened Mississippi Territory. Armed with axes, kettles, and most importantly their Bibles, the early pioneers of Alabama faced an environment such as they had never known before, but they stayed and built their homes and survived.

Most of what would become the future State of Alabama was still part of the Mississippi Territory at the end of the 18th century. Except for the Native Americans, the land was still an immense wilderness and sparsely settled by white men.

On April 2, 1799 Winthrop Sargeant, the first governor of the Mississippi Territory, divided the Natchez District into two counties Adams and Pickering. The names were chosen to honor the President of the United States and the Secretary of State. There was not more than five thousand people residing in the Mississippi Territory at this time.

In the Natchez District on the Tombigbee and Mobile Rivers which later became part of the state of Alabama, the population only consisted of around eight hundred inhabitants, most of whom were Anglo-Americans. Some had been residents of the British colonies of West Florida and were of Spanish and French descent. Others were loyalists emigrants from the United States who had traveled to the region prior to and after the Revolutionary War with inducements held out by the Spanish governor before 1792.

Fort Charlotte at Mobile was still garrisoned with Spanish troops as late as 1792. The old French 'Tombecbe' which in Spanish times was called Port Confederation, also contained a Spanish garrison. The English trading post Tensaw near present day Stockton, Alabama was repaired and occupied.

A Spanish garrison occupied Fort St. Stephens, (in present day Washington County, Alabama) which had been built upon a bluff on the Tombigbee. It was called Hobuckintopa by the Choctaws. Another Spanish garrison held the fortress at Pensacola while West Florida and Louisiana were governed by the Captain-General at Havana.

The next person in authority was the Governor of Louisiana, to whom all the commandants of the posts in Alabama and Mississippi were subordinate. With American trading-posts on the east on the Oconee, Spain upon the south and west, and few settlements in the distant Cumberland settlements in the north, much of the central part of the future state of Alabama was largely uninhabited by whites.

As the settlers arrived, they brought their institutions and peculiar forms of thought and traditions with them. Each pioneer came with the hope of finding a better life in the Mississippi Territory.

Visit http://alabamapioneers.com
for more unknown stories about the state of Alababama and follow on Facebook at
http://www.facebook.com/alabamapioneers
and
http://twitter.com/alabamapioneers

Table of Contents

Alabama Pioneers Overcame Many Obstacles 1
   In Search Of A Peaceful Life..3
   For Lack Of A Shoemaker..11
   Restless, Wrecked, Rovers..13
   Diary Of Traveling To Alabama In Early 1800s.............................15
   The Trackless Wilderness Of South Alabama 23
   1814 Description Of Native Americans..27
Mississippi Territory..31
   The Yazoo Land Fraud..33
   Citizens Rise Up Against The Governor..37
Dangerous Roads in the Mississippi Territory.....................................43
   Treaties Formed With The Indians For Roads................................45
   Immigrants Bring Their Prejudices To Mississippi Territory...........47
   Natchez Trace And The Federal Road, Most Important Roads In Alabama..51
   Notorious Robber Strikes Fear In The Hearts Of Early Pioneers...55
   Spanish Difficulties Develop..57
   First Counties Established..61
Famous Pioneers Of Early Alabama...65
   Vice-President Aaron Burr Charged With Treason.........................67
   Vice-President Arrested In Alabama...71
   Hero Of The Alamo Kills An Alabama Man..................................85
Fear Of War With The Native Americans Looms Ahead....................89
   Man Killed By Indians – War Threat..91
   Every Free White Male – 16 to 50 Was Subject To Serve In the Militia..97
   Margaret Eades – Witness To Indian Wars.....................................99
   Tecumseh Arrives - Described By A Witness...............................105

Alabama Pioneers Overcame Many Obstacles

In Search Of A Peaceful Life

As early as 1777, some expeditionary trips by hopeful settlers took place in what is now Madison County in north Alabama.

1893 base map of Alabama by Jedediah Hotchkiss with circle of location of Madison County, Alabama

These early pioneers were men who had fought the Native Americans in western Georgia and Middle Tennessee and were use to the danger, privation and suffering of pioneer life. Families from Tennessee and the Carolinas had been subjected to almost constant harassment by the Native Americans.

Finally, the patience of the settlers was completely exhausted and they become gradually stronger. The settlers determined to strike a blow which would reach the heart of the enemy, and to pursue them to their stronghold at Nickajack, where the Cherokees, with their allies, were accustomed to make their incursions.

With much secrecy, General James Robertson led a force of six hundred men to the north bank of the Tennessee River after dark. The men constructed small rafts for their guns and ammunition, and then pushed the rafts before them, sometimes wading and sometimes swimming. They reached the southern bank early the next morning, surrounded their enemies, and gained an overwhelming victory. The power of the tribe was completely broken and the Cherokees for the first time sued for peace. (Saunders)

According to Judge Taylor author of *EARLY HISTORY OF MADISON COUNTY And, Incidentally of North Alabama,* though they were surrounded by Native Americans, there was never a war or major disturbance in the early days of Madison County in North Alabama after the attack at Nickajack.

Judge Taylor reported the only incidents of trouble after Nickajack was an occassion thievery such as a horse taken by Native Americans, but nothing occurred of great import. He related the following incident that took place in 1806 as an example.

Isaac Criner's and his brother's horses were carried off by Native Americans so the two men set out and traveled through the wilderness toward the Native American town of Gunter's village, (now Guntersville) in order to retrieve their property. Once the horses were found, the Native Americans restored them to their rightful owners without any protest.

When the Creek-Indian War began in 1813, it was the middle and southern portions in the State of Alabama that suffered. Even the Chickasaws and Cherokees of North Alabama who did not remain neutral during the war, formed an alliance with the white population against their fellow Native Americans.

The land that would eventually become Madison County, Alabama "was an Indian hunting ground. They visited in autumn and returned laden with game to their settlements on the Tennessee as winter set in." (Taylor)

This early pioneer period of Madison County extended from 1805 to 1810, and up to the close of the year in 1809 the population was around five thousand. As a general rule, the people were of moderate means who came to northern Alabama to acquire a home and shelter for their families where the land was cheap and the soil fertile.

As the stories of the beauty and fertility of northern Alabama spread, the area began to attract a more cultured and wealthy population. Slaves were brought to Northern Alabama in considerable numbers. (Taylor)

During the first year the pioneers had to bring corn and salt on pack horses through the wilderness. The first settlers near Winchester in Franklin County, Tennesee went to the mill near Shelbyville, Tennessee for bread and the first settlers in Madison County, Alabama had no mills nearer than those in Tennessee.

Location of Winchester, Tennessee (Courtesy National Weather Service -Huntsville, Alabama)

Since it was a difficult journey to Tennesse, they were often without bread or salt for days and subsisted on jerked venison.

The settlers planted and cultivated a corn patch for bread, but since they did not have a local mill to ground the corn, they had to come up with another solution. A hominy mortar was constructed by burning or digging out a large bowl in the end of a large stick of hard tough timber in which they pounded their corn with the use of a large pestle worked by a sweep. (Taylor)

Wood ash was also used to make a corn crop, lye-hominy as a substitute for bread. Wheat flour was a rare commodity as it was not locally grown for many years and had to be brought down the Tennessee River in large quantity to Ditto's landing. There a "flour inspector was appointed to inspect, grade and stamp the flour before it was offered for sale." (Taylor)

Hunters or explorers in the forest subsisted on parched corn or animals they killed. Meat could be acquired in abundance, but since salt could only be obtained from Nashville by pack horses, it was difficult to preserve the fresh meat. Later flat boats from Virginia and Tennessee were used to transport salt.

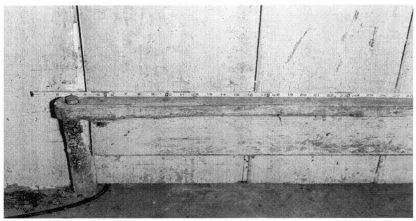

Typical Wooden Hinge used on door at basement level in the Isaac Hammer House, Johnson City, Washington County, TN 1793 log single-dwelling (Historic American Buildings Survey – Library of Congress)

Iron was not available and doors swung on wooden hinges with wooden locks for many years.

Since wood was in abundance, it was used everywhere. "The floors of the rooms were dirt or made of puncheons; the boards were laid on the roof and held fast by weight poles laid on each course, the lowest pole pegged down and the others separated and kept in position by timber pieces between them." (Taylor) Even bread trays, bowls and tableware were made from buckeye, basswood and other soft timber.

Pewter was sometimes available and wives scoured their pewter plates "until they shone like silver and set them edge-wise on shelves across which a slat was pegged and when tastefully arranged, they made quite a showy display." (Taylor) Tinkers traveled from house to house to repair and mend the family pewter. Money was scarce so the tinkers often bartered for needed items.

The old fashioned long rifle with flintlock was the universal weapon for hunting. Shot guns were not in use, and as lead was essential they never wasted it and generally managed to keep a supply. (Taylor)

When gun powder was scarce, the pioneers were equal to the difficulty. Sulphur was easily procured and they constructed hoppers in the mountain caves and made saltpetre. Willow was burned for charcoal and made into gun-powder. Though it may not have been as good and reliable, it served their purpose. The men were expert in the use of the rifle, and it was not considered an extraordinary feat to bring down a deer at full speed at a distance of seventy-five or eighty yards. (Taylor)

Dressed buckskin was used for bed covering, garments, moccasins, sacks and hunting pouches, and thongs for sewing as well as twisted into ropes. Flax was sown to make cloth from flax wheels. When cotton was introduced, the spinning wheel and cards, the loom, as well as winding blades and reel became common in every settler's house.

Early pioneers did not have a cotton gin and seeds had to be removed by hand. Long winter evenings were spent in front of the fire with a pile of cotton nearby which the whole family cleaned by picking the seeds out with their fingers.

Pegs inserted in the walls of the room were usually hung with great festoons or bunches of "hanks" of home spun thread ready for warping, bars and loom. The cloth made from this material was heavy in body and almost impervious to the assault of the bushes and brambles with which the wearers came in daily contact.

The bark of various forest trees as well as coperas, indigo and madder (a red dye from the madder plant) was used as dye to color the cotton. Calico was almost unknown and was worth fifty cents a yard so it was seldom worn by common people. The young ladies wore home spun dresses and buckskin moccasins.

House furniture had to be made as well and was of the rudest character. Cabins were without glass, and "cooking utensils were few in number; tallow, rosin and beeswax was used for light in the evenings." (Taylor)

The earliest pioneers in Alabama used bear's grease in their home-made lamps, but when cattle became common, they had molded or dipped tallow candles with a cotton wick.

In summer, the families retired early and seldom used a light unless someone was ill. Some people constructed a cotton wick fifteen or twenty feet long, then dipped it in beeswax and rosin, wound it around a corn cob and drew the wick through the aperture made by burning out the pith of the cob and pulled it up as it burned. This made the taper last a long time.

In primitive times, houses were usually small, but families were often large, so they used curtains of buckskin to divide the cabin into sleeping quarters.

Little children often slept on pallets on the floor, while the larger boys climbed a step-ladder to a loft above. "The boys of that day loved the open air and were not very particular about a roosting place. They would sleep on a scaffold under the trees in the yard, or in the stable loft, and frequently would go off on a night hunt and after the sport was over would build a fire and sleep in the woods." (Taylor)

For Lack Of A Shoemaker

"Notwithstanding the luxuriant abundance of natural elements, with which the early settlers found themselves surrounded, they were not exempt from the privations then universally incident to pioneer life. Vast forests had to be felled, and the fields to be cultivated, but most scanty was the supply of implements with which the formidable task had to be undertaken; and the few in hand were of the rudest character. A few axes and grubbing hoes, such as the daring emigrants had brought with them from their distant homes, were the only utensils that could be brought into practical requisition." (Riley)

With the heroism that prompted pioneers to penetrate the forest wilds, they energetically addressed themselves to a stupendous task. At every step, they encountered new difficulties; once a problem was overcome, another was introduced. By dint of arduous and tedious toil, the forests were partially cleared away, but what were the implements of agriculture with which the soil was to be tilled?

"A few shovels, spades and grubbing hoes, of the rudest character, and an occasional scooter plow, were the only implements with which these primitive agriculturists were to raise their virgin crops. The only instrument used by many of the wealthiest farmers, for several years, was a sharply-flattened hickory pole, made somewhat in the shape of a crowbar, with which holes were made in the soil and the seed deposited." (Riley) An embarrassing difficulty arose from the absence of smithy facilities among the early farmers, and they saw but little hope of relief for their problem until one immigrated to the new Territory.

One of the severest privations to which the pioneer families were subjected was a great scarcity of shoes. Many of the fathers and grandfathers of the influential families were, from necessity, 'barefoot laborers'.

"The early soil was tilled, through heat and cold, by bare-footed men. The game was chased over the hills by men wearing no shoes. Men and women taught school, and attended church, with feet totally unprotected. And to show that it was not incompatible with primitive dignity, one of the earliest aspirants to Legislative honors, Captain Cumming actively canvassed the county of Conecuh, on horseback, with his feet clad only in their native nudeness. It is said to have been not an infrequent occurrence to meet men, on horseback, with their naked feet armed with a pair of rude wooden spurs."

Restless, Wrecked, Rovers

Some early permanent settlers in Clarke County, Alabama came from Georgia, which had been colonized in 1733. They had traveled from the Carolinas, colonized between 1640 and 1670, from Virginia, where the first English settlement commenced in 1607. Others settling in Clarke County came from Kentucky, which had been settled by six families led by Daniel Boone in 1773. The six families were joined by forty others from Powell's Valley, and constituted all the white settlers of Kentucky in 1773.

Still more came from Tennessee, where temporary settlements were made in 1765, but the important and permanent ones not until 1774. These Tennessee settlers had lived independent of North Carolina or the United Colonies till 1788, when their country was ceded to Congress and they became a part of the state of North Carolina.

"Americans, so soon as they began to be American citizens, manifested that roving, restless nature, which makes them probably the most migratory of all the great and enlightened nations. Scarcely, it would seem were the fruits of cultivation beginning to be enjoyed, in these certainly new states, before many enterprising, brave, and daring pioneers are ready to enter upon what was then the last acquired territory of the Union." (Ball)

McIntosh Bluff was an English-grant, the tract of land so-called having been given by the King of England to Captain John McIntosh who was connected with the army of West Florida. John McIntosh had a son who became a British officer, and a daughter born in Georgia. This daughter went to England, married a British offficer named Troup, returned to Mobile, and went up the river in a barge to her father's residence. There, in 1780, at McIntosh Bluff, was born a son who bore the name of George M. Troup and who became in after years a distinguished governor of Georgia, one of the vigorous political writers of his age.

The McIntosh family were Scotch highlanders, and while one branch had its representatives in the British army, other members of the family, citizens of Georgia, were zealous whigs during the Revolution. Among these were Colonel John and General Lachlan McIntosh, the latter having come to the Georgian colony when a boy with Oglethorpe, its founder.

At McIntosh Bluff was held the first County Court of Washington county, in 1803. Thomas Malone became clerk of the court of Washington County, Alabama with John Caller, Cornelius Rain, and John Johnson presiding.

Diary Of Traveling To Alabama In Early 1800s

Margaret Eades was the wife of Jeremiah Austill of the Legendary Canoe Fight that took place during the Creek-Indian War in Alabama. She, like her husband, was an early pioneer of Alabama. Mrs. Austill died in 1890 having borne several children. In the excerpt from her autobiography below she relates her experiences as a pioneer family in Clarke County, Alabama.

Note: *This has been transcribed exactly as written with misspellings, etc.*

My father, John Eades, was a native of Georgia, my mother, Jenny Fee, was born in Ireland, in the County Atmah. Father and Mother first met in Augusta, Georgia, where they were married in 1802. They then left Augusta and bought a farm in Washington County on the Uchee Creek, where they lived happily and made money rapidly.

Father had a saw mill and cotton gin, about the first one that was put up in the County. I well remember the mode of packing cotton in that early day. A round bag was fixed in a round hole in the floor of the gin house, which hung down some ten feet. A big negro man jumped in with an iron crowbar, two hands threw in the cotton, and the packer did the work by jambing it hard with an awful grunt every lick. I was dreadfully afraid to go near the big bag with the negro inside shaking it.

Oh, it was a sad day when Father determined to move to Louisiana, but so it was, that on a bright morning in the spring of 1811, the wagons were loaded and three families were assembled at my Father's house. My Uncle, Daniel Eades, his wife and one daughter, Mr. Billy Locklin and wife, and about one hundred slaves, men, women and children, and with much weeping at parting from dear old friends, the drivers cracked their whips and off we rolled, much to my delight. But my sister, five years older than myself, was weeping bitterly.

I was all talk, she said to me "Do hush, you too will rue the day." Childlike, I reveled in a bustle and change.

Well, the first night we camped at Sweetwater Iron Works, where Father's sister, Mrs. Jenkins, came to bid us good-bye. She was a jolly old soul—was Aunt Priscilla. She spent the night with us in camp, after breakfast next morning she drew put a flask of rye rum from her pocket, saying "John and Daniel, I drink to all, good luck attend you, but the next thing I hear will be that you all have been scalped by the savages, so be on your guard, for war will surely come, and that soon. Farewell, may the Lord guide you through the wilderness."

Our party traveled on through the Cherokee Nation without the least trouble. The Indians were kind and friendly, but as soon as we entered the Creek or Muskogee Nation, we could see the terrible hatred to the white, but as we advanced, we were joined by many movers, which gave us more security.

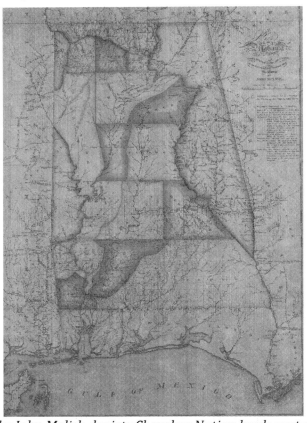

1820 map by John Melish depicts Cherokee Nation lands east of Alabama (Library of Congress)

At night the wagons were all fixed round the encampment, the women and children and negroes in the center, the men keeping guard with guns, so we made a formidable appearance of defense.

One night after a fearful day, the Indians had followed us for miles, we camped in an old field. Just as supper was announced, a most terrific earthquake took place, the horses all broke loose, the wagon chains jingled, and every face was pale with fear and horror. The Indians came in numbers around us looking frightened, and grunting out their prayers. The trees lapped together, and Oh, the night was spent in terror by all, but next day some of the Indians came to us, and said it was Tecumseh stamped his foot for war.

Then the rain set in, not a day without rain until we crossed the Alabama, there were no roads, and mud and water large creeks to cross with slender bridges made by the Indians, which they demanded toll at a high price for every soul that crossed a bridge, and often rather than pay, the men would make their negroes cut trees and make a bridge, which gave the Indians great anger, and they would threaten us with death.

No doubt we would have been killed had it not been for Uncle Daniel Eades, who had been stolen from the Fort in Georgia by the very people that threatened us. He was a little boy, only a year old when the Indians took him from the nurses and carried him to the Nation, and gave him as a present to their big Medicine Man, who raised him and taught him his craft in roots and herbs.

He would talk to them and defy them, he would go to his wagon and draw out Grandfather's long sword that he wore in the Revolution, brandish the sword, and speak to them in their own language, telling them they were fools, that they were nothing, and could never whip the whites, but that their Nation would be destroyed. They would listen to him, and raised their blankets around their shoulders and move off, doggedly shaking their heads.

Well, finally we crossed the Alabama River at Bale's Ferry, we then were in Clarke County, bound for Louisiana, expecting to cross the Tombigbee next day at Carney's Ferry. That night we camped at this place, some of the neighbors came to see us, Mr. Joel Carney, Mr. Henry B. Slade, Mr. George S. Gullet, and every one begged Father and all the travelers with him to stop here until they could recruit their teams that were completely broken down. They said we could never get through the swamp on the other side of Bigbee, and after a consultation, all consented to remain until they could make corn to fatten their teams.

1893 map Clarke County, Alabama (Library of Congress)

Father bought this place, which was only a claim with a small log cabin on it. Daniel Eades rented the Sun Flower Bend, Billy Locklin built a cabin on Salt Creek, and put up a saw and grist mill on the creek in a very short time, the first saw mill that was built in Clarke County. So Father put some hands to cutting cane and planted corn. He had brought a whip saw with him, he put up large logs of pine on a scaffold, and with two negroes, one on top and one at the bottom.

They sawed planks for flooring, for every family then lived in cabins on ground floors. Father kept on building and making us comfortable, but when the corn was gathered, Uncle Daniel Eacles said, "Well, John, it is time to be off, let us hurry up and be gone, the waters are low, the roads good, the teams fat, and all well. This is no country for us, let us travel."

Father said, "Daniel, I am getting fixed up here, the water is splendid, the land good enough, and you have made a fine crop of corn, we have wild game plenty for the shooting, and I can't see that we could do better."

"John," he replied, "You will never make a fortune here, so come with me, I hate to leave you, but here I will not stay." But Father would not leave, so Uncle Daniel left, and we only had one year of peace, for the Indians came down upon us with vengeance. Uncle Daniel came back for us, said everything he could to get Father to go with him, but all in vain, so he left us to battle through the fearful war.

Part II

One morning, Mother, Sister, and myself were at home alone except the servants, Father had gone to the plantation, when a man rode up to the gate and called to Mother to fly, for the Creek Indians had crossed the Alabama, and were killing the people.

Mother said, "Where shall I fly to, in God's name?"

He said, "There are a number of people coming to cross the Bigbee to get into the Choctaw Nation, they will be along in a few moments, but where is Captain Eades?"

"Down at the river," said Mother.

"Well," he said, "Run, down there and go over the river."

So we took our bonnets, Mother took her silver, and we left the house in a run.

Our cook, a tall black handsome woman, said "Missus, I will stay at home and take care of things and take you something to eat if I can find you, the devils are afraid of me, you know."

Mother said, "Hannah, you will be murdered."

Hannah was a natural curiosity, she was black, or rather blue-black, with clear blue eyes, which gave her a peculiar appearance. As we traveled through the Nation the Indians often came to the camp and demanded bread, they would say "bread, gimme some, gimme all."

Mother would say to Hannah to give them bread, she would say, "I had rather give them shot and powder," then she would stretch her blue eyes and throw chunks of fire at them, and make them scamper off, saying "Och, och," their grunt when frightened.

Well we ran as fast as we could, and met Father about a mile from home with horses, he had heard the news too. Mother sent the horses on to help a family by the name of Carter to get to the river, they had a large family of small children.

Father told us that people were gathering at Carney's Bluff; and were at work there building a Fort, all hands, negroes and whites. When we arrived at the river it was a busy scene, men hard at work chopping and clearing a place for a Fort, women and children crying, no place to sit down, nothing to eat, all confusion and dismay, expecting every moment to be scalped and tomahawked.

We all sat round until night, people coming in continually, for this part of Clarke was thickly settled, I went to Mother and told her I was tired and sleepy, she untied her apron and spread it down on the ground, and told me to say my prayers and go to sleep, so I laid me down, but could not sleep, the roots hurt me so badly. I told Mother I had rather jump in the river than lie there, she quietly replied, "Perhaps it would be best for us all to jump in the river," then made me lie still. I had thought Mother would take me on her lap if I was so willing to die.

With super-human exertion, the Fort was finished in one week, the tents all comfortable, the streets full of soldier boys drilling, drums beating, pipes playing, but no Indians yet. Our scouts were out all the time. The brave fellows had a hard time tramping through swamps and canebrakes, but Oh, after the war did set in in Thirteen, we were in great peril all the time.

The Trackless Wilderness Of South Alabama

"White settlers from other states began to settle on the lower 'Bikbee (Tombigbee) around 1790. They came very slowly, however, and numbered only twelve hundred and fifty souls ten years later when a census was taken."

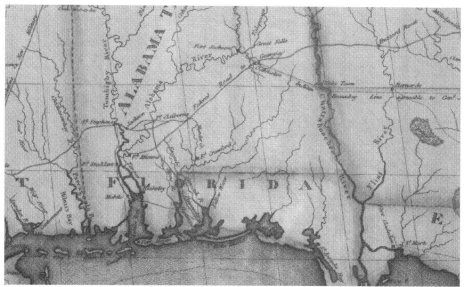
1810 map with Tombigbee settlement area, Alabama (Library of Congress)

The trackless wilderness that lay between was fraught with obstacles and perils that none but the boldest dared to encounter. This area in 1800 comprised the first county of the southern part of the Mississippi Territory and was named Washington. (Brewer)

In February, 1791, a party of emigrants, consisting of Colonel Thomas Kimbel, John Barnett, Robert Sheffield, Barton Hannon, and Mounger, with a wife and children, three of whom were grown, set out from Georgia for the Tombigbee.

Entering the Creek nation, one of the children was injured by a fall, which compelled the elder Mounger and his younger family to stop upon the trail. They were afterwards robbed by the Indians of everything they possessed, and had to make their way back to Georgia on foot. The three young Moungers, and the other emigrants, continued to the Tensaw, passing the creeks and rivers upon rafts.

"They found upon their arrival at Tensaw the Halls, Byrnes, Mims, Kilcreas, Steadhams, Easlies, Linders and others. Crossing the Alabama and Tombigby (Tombigbee) upon rafts, they found residing below McIntosh Bluff, the Bates, Lawrences, and Powells. Above there, on the Tombigby, they discovered the Danley, Wheets, Johnsons, McGrews, Hockets, Freelands, Talleys, and Bakers."

"Among these few people, Colonel Kimbrel and his little party established themselves, and began the cultivation of the soil with their horses, upon the backs of which they had brought a few axes and ploughs."

The garrison at St. Stephens in Washington County was composed of one company commanded by Captain Fernando Lisoro. The block house, the residence of the commandant and the church, were good buildings, of frame-work, clay and plaster. The other houses were small, and covered with cypress bark.

All the inhabitants were required to labor so many days upon the public works, to take the oath of allegiance, and to assist in repelling the depredations of the Creeks, who stole horses and other property.

Some French farmers also lived upon this river, who dwelt in houses made almost entirely of clay, while those of the Americans were constructed of small poles in the rudest manner. They all cultivated indigo, which was worth two dollars and fifty cents per pound. The burning of tar engaged much of the time of the Spaniards who lived closer to the Gulf.

"Upon Little river, dividing the modern counties of Baldwin and Monroe, lived many intelligent and wealthy people, whose blood was a mixture of white and Indian. This colony was formed at an earlier period to benefit the their large stocks of cattle that fed on the wild grass and cane which was never killed by the frost."

1814 Description Of Native Americans

In 1792, there were no white settlements between the Alabama river and northward in the vicinity of Nashville except for the old French settlement of Fort Toulouse. This major part of this area was inhabited by the Creeks.

The following description is from Stephen D. Ray, who lived among the Native Americans in Alabama around 1814 until they were removed. This description is included in George Brewer's, *History of Coosa County* and provides us with some indication as to their appearance and habits of Native Americans in the central part of the state of Alabama from his personal perspective. It may differ from Native Americans in other parts of the the state of Alabama.

Clothing

The garb of the men was a hunting shirt that reached to the knees, with raw-hide leggings that reached to the hips from his feet. The hair was cut close to the skin of his head, with a roach from his forehead to the back of his neck. He wore no hat.

The female dress was a jacket with sleeves, which reached to her hips, and a skirt from her hips to her feet. They went bare-headed, and bare-footed, and their hair floated loose around their shoulders.

Diet

Their diet, in part, was soup made of corn, parched and then pounded into meal, boiled in an earthen pot. They sat on the ground around the pot, and ate from it with a spoon, one spoon serving for all, as each one would dip by turns and drink.

The spoon would hold about as much as a tea cup. There was no salt or other seasoning in the soup.

Family Relationships

These Indians make beasts of burden of their wives. When they go to market among the whites, she carries the produce such as corn, potatoes, berries, fruits or other things in a basket fastened to her shoulders. If he owns a horse he rides and carries nothing. The wife, however, seems to think it an honor to thus wait on her man.

The Indian man is the most indolent of human beings. He seems naturally averse to labor. His wife and daughters do all the work on the farm, digging it up, planting, and cultivating it with the hoe, a very poor one at that, while he lies up and sleeps, or is off on the hunt or war-path.

Their way of approaching the house of a white person is peculiar. When they get in sight of the house and near, they sit down in the road or path, and wait, even for hours, for some one from the house to invite them in. If no one comes, they get up and march on.

The Green Corn Dance

The Indians hold what we call a Green Corn Dance, once each year, about the time corn gets into the roasting-ear stage. It lasts about three days and nights, and they fast all that time. The chief sits on a raised embankment, with a drum, often made of an earthen pot covered with a raw-hide head, and one stick with which he taps on the drum, while the warriors, some hundreds in number, in single or double file move around him, dancing and keeping time to his drum.

This is an act of religious worship to the Great Spirit, and a degree of profound solemnity is observed through all of it. The last day they take the "black drink," which is a dark tea made from some herb (yaupon), which is very bitter, and bring on nausea, producing violent vomiting. They claim this purges from the sins of the past year, and prepares them to enter the new year clean.

This is followed by a feast. The women come from all directions with baskets loaded with corn, boiled in the shuck, with pumpkins unpeeled, boiled whole, other vegetables, with meats, all without salt or other seasoning. All participate in the feast, and thus ends their most solemn religious season.

Brewer in *History of Coosa County* also tells of a diary owned by an early Coosa County pioneer named Joel Spigener in which he states the following about an Indian ball play he attended in the company of Charles Bulger in July 1833.

This play was about two miles above Hatchesofka Creek, on the Jackson Trace road as afterwards established. These two were the only whites present. There were more than four hundred Indians. He says he never saw anything to equal the expertness with which they played. The balls would fly higher than the tallest pines. The play lasted about six hours. He and Bulger bet fifty cents on one party, but did not know they had won until the stake holder handed them the money.

He attended the green-corn dance at Jabouver Town House, five miles above Wetumpka, in 1834. The name of the presiding chief was Magilberree. At this dance a young man named Brown was killed by another man named Houghton. Brown's parents lived in Georgia, and Houghton's in Wetumpka.

At the green-corn dance of July 1835, at Alabama Town, Joel Spigener and his whole family attended. He said it was a very solemn religious rite. "The Indians insisted on his daughter Eliza and Miss Caroline Paulden, a niece, to participate in the dance. They accepted, and went through the dance just like the Indian squaws. The chief of Alabama Town at the time of this dance was Sukabitchee, or Broadback."

Mississippi Territory

The Yazoo Land Fraud

When peace finally came between the United States and Great Britain, the colonists acquired the territory east of the Mississippi and north of the 31st latitude. Spain disputed the United States claim south of the latitude of 30-28 and only released the claim after Gen. Thomas R. Pinkney visited Madrid in 1795. Spain continued to hold some control of the disputed territory until 1798.

There was an tremendous rush of people to the West after the Revolutionary War. The state of Georgia immediately asserted her ownership to the immense region between the Chattahoochee River and the Mississippi River which included the future State of Alabama and began to make preparations for colonization.

In 1785, a party of settlers set out into the wilds of Alabama to organize counties. First, they organized the portion all the portion of Alabama lying north of the Tennessee river into a county they named Houston after Governor John Houston of Georgia. Muscle Shoals was the first seat of government in this county. Houston did not remain a county for long due to slow immigration and the early settlers fear of the Indians in the wilds of Alabama. The settlement was abandoned and the party returned to Georgia.

Since it was difficult and dangerous for settlers to go alone to the newly acquired land, an excellent opportunity became available for land speculators to gain control of large bodies of land, organize companies of people who wanted to migrate, and thus secure permanence and safety to the new settlements, and incidentally make huge profits on the land they sold to settlers.

Four land companies in the state of Georgia in 1789 were organized for the purpose of buying from Georgia parts of the western territory of the United States. The land which they desired to obtain was in the neighborhood of the Yazoo River, and on that account the companies were called Yazoo Companies.

The United States government claimed all of the western territory, but Spain was in still in actual possession of part of the Yazoo land so it was easy to persuade the Georgia legislature to sell any claim the state had in the land. The Yazoo Company succeeded in acquiring deeds to 14,400,000 acres for the insignificant price, $207,580.

"In 1795, President Washington discountenanced the sale of western lands to settlement promoters, on the ground that the states had no right to sell lands in the possession of the Indians without first buying their rights, and because it was feared that colonies planted so close to New Orleans might come under the control of Spain."

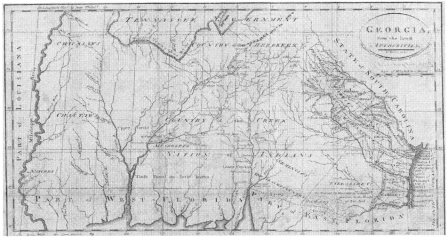
1795 map reveals Native American Land (Library of Congress)

There was a great deal of dissatisfaction at that time among the Americans who had settled on the Mississippi River, on account of the fact that Spain controlled the Mississippi and would not allow them to use the river for their commerce.

Indeed, Spain tried to detach the western settlements from their allegiance to the United States by offering to give them the right to use the river if they would become Spanish subjects.

In spite of these objections, the Yazoo Land Company made a concerted effort to secure possession of western land. James Gunn, a United States Senator from Georgia was the leader of this group. Their scheme was successful and the legislature granted the company 40,000,000 acres of land, for about $500,000. The state gave no guarantee against Spanish claims and was not to be held responsible for peace with the Native Americans.

Later information yielded that "a small body of twenty senators and thirty-four representatives were bribed to make the sale through the means of gifts, money or shares in the land companies."

It was said that, "In the lobbies of the Senate and House alternately were seen a judge of the Supreme Court of the United States, from Pennsylvania, with twenty-five thousand dollars in his hands as a cash payment; a judge of the United States District Court of Georgia passing off shares of land to the members for their votes, and a senator from Georgia [Gunn], who had perfidiously neglected to proceed to Philadelphia to take his seat in Congress, and who was absent form his post until the last days of its session, bullying with a loaded whip, and by turns cajoling the numerous understrappers in speculation."(Brooks)

"Even before the governor signed the act, there were indications of popular disapproval. A number of prominent citizens protested against the measure, William H. Crawford among others. Governor Matthews was strongly censured for signing the bill." (Brooks)

A state convention met soon after the passage of the Yazoo act and condemned the sale, and it became the issue in the elections the next year. General James Jackson, one of Georgia's U. S. senators, felt so strongly about the act that he resigned his seat in the Senate and returned home to lead a movement to repeal the act.

A rescinding measure was passed in February, 1796 and the purchase money paid into the Treasury of Georgia was ordered to be refunded.

People throughout the United States began to voice their anger over the act so the Yazoo speculators, after receiving their grants, fled to other sections of the country where they were able to sale their holdings to unaware purchasers at enormous profit.

Then, Georgia followed other states at this time and surrendered all her western claims to the United States government for which she received $1,250,000. The Indian title to her reserved territory was extinguished and the Yazoo Fraud became a national issue.

Yazoo claimants swarmed to Washington declaring that they owned the land Georgia ceded to the government and for a number of years, Congress was besieged with petitions from people seeking redress. Representatives of Georgia, of whom the future 1st governor of Alabama, William W. Bibb, was one, firmly opposed any appropriation to settle the claims.

A commission was formed to look into the Yazoo matter in 1803. Their report stated that all the lands had passed out of the hands of the original speculators and on the face of the deeds a provision declared that purchasers should have no claim against the speculators 'by reason of any defect in their title from the State of Georgia' thus making their claims invalid.

The commission was concerned about the tranquility of those who inhabited the new lands so they urged recommended that $5,000,000 be appropriated to settle the claims and end the controversy. Congress did not share their view and did not appropriate the funds.

Finally, the case was taken to the Supreme Court and Chief Justice Marshall handed down the decision which held that the rescinding act was unconstitutional in that it impaired the validity of a contract.

Following this decision Congress passed an act in 1814 that appropriated $5,000,000 to settle all Yazoo claims. The act required that the money should be raised from sales of the land in question.

Citizens Rise Up Against The Governor

In 1798, Congress created the Mississippi Territory that included the portions of Alabama and Mississippi east and west along the northern boundary of Florida from the Chattahoochee to the Mississippi Rivers and south between the two rivers a little north of Montgomery. Natchez, on the Mississippi, was authorized as the seat of government.

Winthrop Sargeant was appointed governor of the new Mississippi Territory May 7, 1798 by President Adams. When Sargeant arrived in Natchez Aug. 6, 1798, he was very ill. After he recovered, on Aug 16, 1798, he delivered an address to the people of the territory.

Governor Winthrop Sargeant (Library of Congress)

Territorial officers appointed by President Adams were William McGuire, Chief Justice, Judge Peter Bryan Bruin and Daniel Tilton, members of the Court. John Steele was appointed Secretary. Legislative authority was given to the Judges and Governor but Judge Peter Bryan Bruin was the only resident member. Judge Tilton arrived Jan 10, 1799 and Judge McGuire arrived the summer of 1800.

Since France and the United States were on the eve of hostilities at this time, Sargeant temporarily organized the militia Sept. 8, 1798.

There was discontent among the people under the leadership of Anthony Hutchins and Col. Cato West (*Westville in Simpson County, Mississippi is named for Cato West) and since Sargeant was a Federalist and the majority of the people were Jeffersonian-Republicans, it was difficult for Sargeant to govern the territory.

When Judge Tilton arrived, the legislature was organized and the first law passed occurred Feb. 28, 1799.

The people continued to protest the laws passed and a public meeting was held to present grievances and to the Governor Sargeant and the Judges. At this meeting a committee of dissenters appointed Narsworthy Hunter as their agent to present their complaints before Congress in Philadelphia.

The petition was prepared by Cato West and had the signature of fifteen citizens of the Mississippi territory. After receiving the petition, Congress on June 24, 1800, authorized a legislative body for the territory "to consist of a House of Representatives elected by the people, and a Legislative Council nominated by the House and the President."

On the 4th Monday in July of 1800 Governor Sargeant authorized an election for members of the House of Representatives. The dissenters overwhelmingly defeated supporters of Governor Sargeant.

The new Representatives met for the first time September 22, 1800. The Mississippi territory was divided into two counties, Adams and Pickering. They were named in honor of President John Adams, General Thomas R. Pickering.

The counties of Adams and Pickering comprised the whole Natchez District until the 4th of June, 1800, when the governor again issued his proclamation, counter-signed by John Steele, secretary, laying off the

"County of Washington" (named in honor of President Washington) on the Tombigbee River. The limits of this county were the territorial boundaries on the north and south, the Pearl River on the west, and the Chattahoochee on the east. The Mississippi Territory was comprised of only these three large counties until the following year.

Adams county (in present state of Mississippi) was represented by Henry Hunter, Anthony Hutchins, James Hogget, and Sutton Banks. Pickering County (later Jefferson County) was represented by Cato West, Thomas M. Green, John Burnet, and Thomas Calvit. The Washington County (in Alabama) election was held irregularly, in that it was not held on the date fixed by law so the House refused to seat its Representative John Flood McGrew.

Pickering and Adams Counties became the Northern part of the territory and bordered what was to later become Madison County. The first Sheriff of Pickering was Lewis Evans while William Ferguson was the Sheriff of Adams.

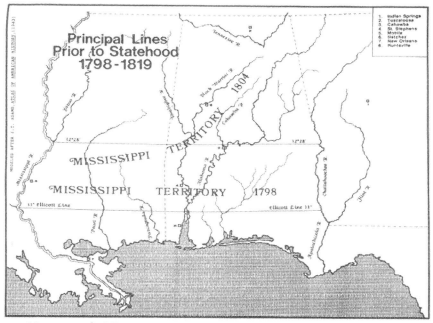

Map reveals Mississippi Territroy in 1798 (Library of Congress)

"The census of 1800 gave the population of the white inhabitants in the entire Mississippi Territory at eight thousand eight hundred and fifty persons. The first census of Washington county was taken in 1800 and found to consist of 733 whites 494 negro slaves and 23 free negroes. The population of Mobile and Baldwin, not then existing as counties, but under Spanish rule, was probably as large, exclusive of about two thousand slaves. In January, 1802, the entire population was probably not less than twelve thousand."

This 2nd form of government of the Mississippi Territory was unpopular by the inhabitants and they petitioned Congress for its repeal Dec. 6, 1800. The petition was signed by 400 citizens of the Mississippi Territory.

When President Adams was defeated by Thomas Jefferson, the settlers of the Mississippi Territory were still dissatisfied with Governor Sargeant's leadership so they petitioned for his removal in 1801.

Governor Sargeant took a leave of absence in April 1801 to visit Washington D. C. in order to defend his administration and to obtain vindication by reappointment but it was to no avail. The petition was granted by President Thomas Jefferson. William Charles Cole Claiborne of Tennessee was appointed Governor Sargeant's successor on May 25, 1801. The new governor, a native of Virginia, possessed much ability.

Charles Claiborne accepted the position, however did not arrive until November 23, 1801 in the Mississippi Territory due to illness. The assembly met in July 1801 and the Territorial Secretary, Colonel John Steele, acted as Governor until Claiborne's arrival. Seth Lewis, a justice of the Territorial Supreme Court wrote Claiborne that Spain had actually agreed to give up Louisiana to France. The secret treaty had been confirmed in March 1801 and it was feared that England would seize New Orleans if the treaty was made known.

When Charles Claiborne arrived, the capital of the Territory was moved to Washington, a village six miles east of Natchez. Claiborne immediately issued rations to the Indians because an Indian had been recently whipped by a citizen and had disappeared so retaliation was feared.

Claiborne asked for an interpreter to deal with the Indians. It was hoped that the rations might help establish friendlier relations with the Indians.

Claiborne gave an address to the Mississippi Territorial Assembly, promising to be fair, cordial and work hard for the common interest as well as improve the judicial system and create the militia. The Assembly was satisfied and some signed a letter stating this. The letter was signed by Henry Hunter, speaker of the House and John Ellis, president of the Council.

Colonel Benjamin Hawkins was an agent to the Creek Indians at Fort Adams and he gave a report from William Dunbar that a conference with the Choctaw Indians was in session and asked that the citizens be friendly to the Indians, especially since the mail must travel through Indian lands.

A treaty with the Choctaws was signed at Fort Adams Dec. 17, 1801. The Choctaws agreed to opening a road through their lands to Tennessee but refused the erection of houses of accommodation. The commissioners of the treaty were Benjamin Hawkins, General James Wilkinson, and Andrew Pickens. The road would be called the Natchez Trace.

White population still came in slowly to the settlement because of the hazards of penetrating the pathless wilderness which lay between the Mississippi Territory and the States. It was also augmented by the presence of the inhospitable Indians in the central part of the future state of Alabama and the difficulty of getting the produce of the country to market.

Additionally, export duties had to be paid at Fort Stoddart to the United States, and a tariff at Mobile had to be paid to Spain. The character of the population was still of the rudest kind, and schools and churches were unknown.

In 1803, emigration from Georgia, Tennessee, and Kentucky, as well as from western Pennsylvania began to augment the population in the old settlements within the five organized counties. Men of capital and enterprise were ready to invest their capital in this valuable land.

However, a large portion of the lands within the limits of the white settlements was still claimed and occupied by virtue of grants or titles derived through the authorities of England, Spain, and Georgia, and required adjudication before confirmation by the United States.

Four fifths of this extensive territory was still in the possession of the Native Americans, comprising about seventy-five thousand souls, and at least ten thousand warriors. The only portions of this territory to which the Native American title had been extinguished was a narrow strip from fifteen to fifty miles in width, on the east side of the Mississippi, and about seventy miles in length, and a small district on the Tombigbee.

Dangerous Roads in the Mississippi Territory

Treaties Formed With The Indians For Roads

In 1799, the only route of intercourse between the Mississippi Territory with the United States was that of the Mississippi and the Ohio Rivers to the settlements of Kentucky and Tennessee; or by the lonely route of a solitary Indian trace, leading for five hundred miles, either to the Cumberland settlements or those of the Oconee in Georgia.

The whole region extending north and east of the Natchez District for nearly five hundred miles, to the settlements on the Cumberland River of Tennessee, and to those on the Oconee, in Georgia, was still Indian territory, in the sole occupancy of the native tribes, except the small district on the Tombigbee and Mobile Rivers. In this location the Indian title had been extinguished by the former governments of France and England.

In 1801, negotiations with the Native American tribes began with the purpose of establishing amicable relations and acquiring consent to open roads and mail-routes from the frontier settlements of Tennessee and Georgia, to those on the Mobile and in the Natchez District.

While at his headquarters at Natchez and Fort Adams, General Wilkinson engaged in negotiations with the Native American tribes south of Tennessee.

The first treaty was held with the Chickasaw nation at Chickasaw Bluff on the Mississippi River in 1801. By this treaty, the Chickasaws conceded to the United States the right of opening a wagon-road from Miro District in Tennessee, to the American settlements in the Natchez District. The agreement stated that this road should be at all times free to the people of the United States passing and repassing from the settlements on the Cumberland River to those near Natchez; also, for the transportation of the United States mail between the same points, free from molestation.

The road crossed at the Tennessee River a few miles below Muscle

Shoals at Colbert's Ferry and led through the Chickasaw Nation to the Grindstone Ford on the Bayor Pierre. The Chickasaws reserved to themselves the privileges and the establishing of public houses for the entertainment of travelers.

The next treaty was with the Choctaw Nation, concluded on the 17th of December, 1801 at Fort Adams. In this treaty, besides other stipulations, the Choctaws consented to the exploration and opening of a convenient wagon-road through their country, from the vicinity of Fort Adams to the Chickasaw boundary near the Yazoo River. The old British boundary which extended from the Tickfaw northwest to the Yazoo, was confirmed and marked anew as the proper boundary between the white settlements and the Native American territory.

This road, communicating with the Chickasaw trace, opened the first direct communication between the settlements on the Lower Mississippi and those of Cumberland near Nashville.

Immigrants Bring Their Prejudices To Mississippi Territory

During the autumn of 1803, numerous emigrants and men of enterprise pressed forward to the Mississippi Territory in anticipation of the final transfer of the province of Louisiana to the United States government. The contemplated occupancy of the area by the United States was expected to take place in December with a ceremony of the national transfer.

Fired with zeal and ardor for the extension of the Federal dominion over the Mississippi valley, hundreds and thousands of merchants, traders, laborers, mechanics, and men of professions, and those in the military— flocked to the area.

Volunteer military companies, fully equipped, coveted the honor of accompanying Federal troops to witness the event. Among the arrivals at Natchez were several volunteer companies of patriotic Tennesseans, impatient of the dominion of Spain. All were eager to witness the glorious termination of the Spanish dominion over the Mississippi.

On the 2nd of December, Governor Claiborne left Natchez in the company of his friends and volunteer troops to join the Federal army under General Wilkinson at Fort Adams. His secreatary, Cato West, remained behind and was in charge of the territorial government in Governor Claiborne's absence. Claiborne's military escort was commanded by Captain Benjamin Farrar, the first troop ever formed in the Mississippi territory.

On the 20th day of December in 1803, the province of Louisiana was formally surrendered to Governor Claiborne. Although the official duties of Governor Claiborne had ceased, he was still the acting governor of the Mississippi Territory until his successor, Robert Williams, would become the governor at the close of the following year.

Louisiana, as surrendered to the United States, embraced only the Island of New Orleans on the east side of the Mississippi, and the Spaniards continued to occupy and exercise dominion over all the remaining country east of the river, and south of the line of demarkation. The port of Mobile, as well as the town and district of Baton Rouge, including one hundred miles of the eastern bank of the river, was still occupied as a portion of West Florida.

In 1804, along the line of demarkation from the Mississippi River eastward to the Chattahoochee River, a distance of more than three hundred miles, the only barrier between the jurisciction and settlements of the Mississippi Territroy and the province of West Florida was an open avenue through the forest, or a surveyor's line and mile-posts through the prairies and open woods.

Governor Charles C. Claiborne (Library of Congress)

The manners and customs, the races and their characteristic traits, their feelings, prejudices, and national antipathies, as well as their government, laws, and civil jurisprudence, were opposite and altogether antagonistical. In such a state, border difficulties between the scattered dwellers occurred frequently. Each placed beyond the reach of the strong arm of the civil authorities, revenged his own wrongs, and vindicated his individual rights.

Border difficulties, broils, and private animosities presented themselves from the first establishment of the line of demarkation so detachments of troops, stationed at intervals along the borders were needed to suppress any important outbreak.

Natchez Trace And The Federal Road, Most Important Roads In Alabama

Most of the Mississippi Territory was still a vast wilderness at the end of the Revolutionary War. Natchez and St. Stephens remained largely isolated from civilization. Natchez communicated with the world by the Mississippi River, while the Tombigbee settlement was separated by the Choctaw Native Americans from the Mississippi River, the Creeks from Georgia, the Cherokees in the mountains of Tennessee, and the Spaniards from the Gulf of Mexico.

The Natchez District extended upon the east side of the Mississippi River for about one hundred miles, and was bounded on the east by a line extending direct from the sources of the the Tickfaw, in a direction west of north to the Yazoo River, ten miles above its mouth. No portion of this district extended more than twenty-five miles direct from the river.

The United States made peace with the Southern Native Americans at the close of the Revolution, and defined their boundaries.

In 1801, after Brigadier-General James Wilkinson, Benjamin Hawkins of North Carolina, and Andrew Pickens of South Carolina, acting as United States commissioners, concluded their treaties with the Chickasaws and Choctaws for the wagon road from the Nashville, Tennessee area to the the Natchez district, work commenced on roads.

One of the roads followed an old trail which crossed the Tennessee River at Muscle Shoals. When it was laid out, it brought a population and civilization to North Alabama and eventually led to the removal of Native Americans from Alabama.

On this road was Doak's Stand which was made famous in treaty annals. Also along this trail, Silas Dinsmore, a Native American agent who cared for the interest of the Choctaws, once defied Andrew Jackson and the Chickasaw Colbert family lived at the Muscle Shoals ferry.

Another trail to Alabama was the old Federal Road which was opened by the United States from the Ocmulgee River in Georgia to Mims' Ferry for St. Stephens in the Mississippi Territory. The Federal Road was opened under Article II of the convention at Washington on November 14, 1805, made by Henry Dearborn, Secretary of War with William McIntosh and other chiefs.

Two years later Harry Toulmin, James Caller and Lemuel Henry, as territorial commissioners extended the Federal Road further west to the capital at Natchez and opened a ferry across the Alabama above Little River and across the Tombigbee above Fort St. Stephens. Prior to this ferry, there had been an older and more used ferry at Nannahubba Island lower down that dated back to 1797.

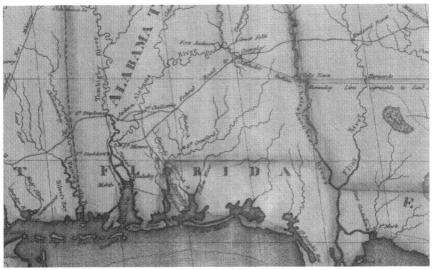

1810 map of Federal road across Alabama St. Stephens to Georgia

A road also ran from Mims' Ferry on the Alabama River to Hollinger's over the Tombigbee, but it was one continuous ferry at high water.

"Causeways were laid over "boggy guts and branches" for the new road and the alternate name for them was "Three Chopped Way" which came from the triple blaze marking from Natchez to Georgia.

The road was mainly a bridle path since it was used principally for horseman and packhorses, but it was also used for one of the oddest vehicles brought by immigrants, the rolling hogshead. Goods were packed in a hogshead, trunions or the equivalent put in the ends, and to them was attached shafts.

"We may suppose horses were generally hitched to this novel affair, but in one instance at least it was an ox, and in this manner many families in 1800 moved to Clarke and other southern counties."

The Federal Road became a wagon road by 1812 according to an early pioneer, Josiah Blakeley. On its route were Fort Mitchell, Fort Bainbridge, Fort Hull, Mount Meigs, Fort Deposit, Burnt Corn, and Fort Montgomery. The road can now be traced only with great difficulty, but without it, there would have been no Alabama as we know it today.

There were other roads in time, but the Federal Road and the Natchez routes were of the most importance in the development and settlement of the future State of Alabama.

Notorious Robber Strikes Fear In The Hearts Of Early Pioneers

After the opening of roads through the wilderness to Tennessee, traders, super-cargoes, and boatmen returned to the northern settlements with the proceeds of their voyage on foot and on horseback. They usually traveled in parties for mutual protection through the Native American Nations, and often rich treasures of specie were packed on mules and horses over these long and toilsome journeys. There was always an ever constant fear of bandits in the back of travelers' minds.

In the year 1802, when all travel and communication from New Orleans and the Mississippi Territory was by way of a solitary trace, or by the slow-ascending barge and keel, a man by the name of Mason made his appearance in the Mississippi Territory.

Accustomed to robbery and murder upon the Lower Ohio, during the Spanish dominion on the Mississippi, and encouraged by the rapid approach of the American population, he left his business of thievery at 'Cave in the Rock', on the Ohio, and began to infest the great Natchez Trace, where the rich proceeds of the river trade was a more tempting prize. He soon became the terror of every peaceful traveler through the wilderness of the Mississippi Territory.

Associated with Mason were his two sons and a few other desperate miscreants. The outrages of Mason and his co-horts became more frequent and saguinary in time. Once he was reported marauding on the banks of the Pearl River, against the life and fortune of a trader, but before a pursuit was organized, a report of another robbery and murder was reported on the remote shores of the Mississippi.

The Mason bandits became so frequent, that the populace was driven to adopt measures for their apprehension. However, the wily bandits baffled every effort of capture.

Finally, a citizen of great respect was passing with his sons through the wilderness and was plundered by the Mason bandits. Luckily the men's lives were spared, but when they returned to the settlement and informed others, the towns people became very angry and pressured the governor of the territory to take action.

Governor Claiborne offered a liberal reward for the robber Mason, dead or alive. The proclamation was widely distributed, and a copy of it reached Mason himself, who was said to "have indulged in much merriment when he received it." However, two of his band were tempted by the large reward, and made a plan to obtain it. When the opportunity arrived, the two conspirators plunged a tomahawk into his brain. They severed his head from his body for identification and took it with triumph to Washington, the seat of justice in the Mississippi Territorial government.

Mason's head was recognized and corresponded with a description as to scars and peculiar markings, but a delay occurred in paying the reward due to the slender state of the treasury. While the two robbers waited in town, many people came to view Mason's head and among the spectators were two young men who had been victims of the bandits. They recognized the companions of Mason as the ones who robbed their father. The robbers were immediately imprisoned, and after the full evidence of their guilt was ascertained, they were condemned and executed at Greenville, in Jefferson County.

Deprived of their leader, the rest of the bandits dispersed and fled the country and the terror that had infested the route through the Native American Nation known as the Natchez Trace was ended.

Spanish Difficulties Develop

In 1805, Congress established the District of Washington in the Mississippi Territory into a revenue precinct, known as the District of Mobile and Fort Stoddart. This District was declared a port of entry for the commerce of the Mobile and Tombigbee settlements. Hence began a series of vexatious exactions, searches, and delays to all American trade or produce passing up or down the river.

The Spaniards at Mobile, twenty miles below the line, claimed the right to control the entire navigation of the bay and river within their limits. They imposed a heavy duty upon all American produce exported, as well as upon all other commodities of trade passing to and from the settlements and the military posts on the river which were located above the line. Even military supplies and Native American annuities from the Federal government were not exempt.

West Florida and Louisiana in 1781 (Library of Congress)

This created a situation where the national government and individual citizens were compelled to pay tribute to a foreign power for the privilege of entering its own ports and navigating its own waters.

The transit duty was levied and collected in the port of Mobile at the rate of twelve and a half per cent ad valorem (by Spanish estimate) upon all articles without exception. Thus the crops destined for the market of New Orleans and the proceeds invested in the necessary articles of domestic use required an aggregate duty of twenty-five per cent for the privilege of passing through the Spanish waters. (American State Papers, Vol. v., P. 94-96)

Every boat and vessel was compelled to pass under the guns of Fort Charlotte and required, on penalty of instant destruction, to make land and submit to a search. Often the whole cargo was overhauled in order to arrive at an estimate, arbitrary in the extreme, in order to affix value for each article for the collection of the imposed revenue. Frequently, vessels were required to unload for the purpose of taking a full inventory of the cargo.

In response to the arbitrary course of the Spanish officers oppressive system, Governor Claiborne sent dispatches August 1805 declaring *that the settlements will be abandoned unless this exaction terminates.*

Before the close of the summer, the border animosities between the American and Spanish population had broken out into acts of open violence and mutual aggression.

The first violation of American soil was on the 12th of August when Lieutenant John Glasscock, with twelve Spanish light-horse, crossed the line two miles into the territory, and forcibly abducted William Flannagan and his wife. They were captured together with horse, saddle, and bridle, fifteen miles into the Spanish dominion; but subsequently finding he had seized the wrong man, Glasscock permitted them to return. However, he retained Flannagan's horse.

Then on the 3rd of September, a border feud ended in an open violation of the American territory by an armed detachment from the Spanish border. Brothers Samuel, Reuben, and Nathan Kemper who resided within the limits of the Mississippi Territory near Pinckneyville had become highly obnoxious to the Spanish authorities and were unlawfully seized at night in their own houses by a party of twelve white men[1] in disguise and seven black men. After personal violence and abusive language, they were taken beyond the line and placed in the custody of a party of twelve Spanish light-horse under the command of Captain Alston who had been waiting to receive them.

The Kemper brothers were hurried off to the river near Tunica Bayou where Captain William Barker and five men took them on board a boat as prisoners to be delivered into the custody of Governor Grandpre at Baton Rouge. However, at daylight, as the boat passed the American post at Point Coupée, the prisoners gave an alarm to a person on shore and before the boat went around the bend, American Lieutenant Wilson crossed the isthmus with a file of soldiers and succeeded in capturing the boat.

The party was sent under guard to the civil authorities at the Washington District. After a hearing before Judge Rodney, they were sent to the Spanish line, and their offense was formally presented to the Spanish governor.

To secure quiet on the border, and to prevent future violations of the American territory, Governor Williams directed two full companies of militia to be stationed near the line, with orders to patrol the country and arrest all trespassers from the Spanish settlements, preserve the peace, and prevent any violation in the Mississippi Territory.

---

1 The disguised white men, who in company with the black men, abducted the Kempers for the Spanish officer, were subsequently ascertained to have been Lewis Ritchie, Minor Butler, Abraham Horton, James Horton, Doctor Bomar, Henry Flowers, Jr and ---- M'Dermont, citizens of the Mississippi Territory, but accessaries and accomplices in the outrage. The guard under Captain Barker, in charge of the prisoners, was composed of Charles Stuart, John Morris, Adam Bingaman, John Ratcliff, and George Rowe, a portion of them being citizens of the Mississippi Territory. (American State Papers, vol v., p. 124

First Counties Established

In 1805, the eastern half of the Mississippi Territory was still an unbroken wilderness in the possession of the Creek Nation, except the district on the Tombigbee and Mobile Rivers. The routes from this district to Georgia and East Tennessee were only Native American trails traveled and occupied by the Creeks and Cherokees. Treaties were negotiated by the Federal Government in 1805 with the Native Americans to open direct communication between settlements.

1796 map of land Indian land and U. S. land

The first treaty was with the Chickasaws and they ceded three hundred and forty-five thousand acres in the extreme eastern portion of their country lying north of the Great Bend of the Tennessee River in the vicinity of Huntsville which later became Madison County.

The next treaty was with the Cherokees at Tellico On October 7, 1805. With this treaty, the United States created a mail-route through the Cherokee Nation from Knoxville to New Orleans by way of the Tellico and the Tombigbee Rivers.

At a treaty concluded on the 14th on November, 1805, about thirty Creek Chiefs guaranteed to the people of the United States a right to a horse-path through the Creek country from the Ocmulgee to the Mobile River.

In consideration of the sum of fifty thousand five hundred dollars and a perpetual annuity of three thousand dollars, and other sums formerly paid, the Indians conveyed their title to the whole territory lying west of Washington county, on the Tombigbee and east of the old Choctaw boundary. With this treaty of Mount Dexter on Nov. 16, 1805, the Choctaws ceded a large district in southern Mississippi, and extending across from the strip on the Mississippi already ceded to that on the Tombigbee, and across that stream to a point near the where later the post office was located in "Choctaw Corner," in the county of Clarke, Alabama, then down the comb of the water shed separating the affluents of the two rivers.

The treaty was signed by James Robertson and Silas Dinsmore, on the part of the federal government, and Puckshenubbee, Homastubbee, Pushmataha, and twenty chiefs and warriors on the part Choctaws with John McKee, William Colbert, the Chickasaw agent Samuel Mitchell, John Pitchlynn, Louis Leflore, Charles Juzant, and others as witnesses.

This was quite an important treaty as the whole southern portion of the present State of Mississippi was thrown open to the white population and the Choctaw Nation was virtually removed from the Spanish border by an intervening strip of more than fifty miles in width.

Out of the Chickasaw cession, Governor Williams created the county of Madison by proclamation in 1808. Already the smoke from the cabin of the whites had begun to ascend from the valley of the Tennessee, and the echo of his axe in those solitudes heralded the onward tramp of white civilization.

Baldwin County was established the west side of the Mobile and Alabama in 1809.

The same year David Holmes of Virginia succeeded Governor Williams. Mobile still remained in the hands of the Spaniards.

In 1810 the three counties lying within the present State of Alabama, Madison, Washington, and Baldwin contained a white population of 6422, and a black population of 2624. A fraction over half of these were in Madison.

Immigration was assisted by a military road which the Muscogees allowed the federal government to cut from the Chattahoochee to Mimms' Ferry, on the Alabama. The three counties sent delegates to the territorial legislature at Washington, Mississippi Territory.

Famous Pioneers Of Early Alabama

Vice-President Aaron Burr Charged With Treason

Aaron Burr, Jr. was the third Vice President of the United States. He served as an officer in the Revolutionary War, then became a successful lawyer and politician. However, when he became Vice President, he and political rival Alexander Hamilton became involved in an illegal duel. Hamilton was killed in the duel. Burr was tried and all charges were dropped against him, but his political career was ended because of the controversy surrounding the duel.

Aaron Burr (Library of Congress)

Burr left Washington D.C and traveled west where he became involved in economic and political activities that led to his arrest on charges of treason in Kentucky. The charges were dismissed and he was released so Burr proceeded to Nashville to stay with numerous friends there. He raised money in Nashville and prepared to travel to Natchez and New

Orleans with three hundred men.

Rumors flew that Burr was organizing a secret expedition against the Spanish provinces and four thousand men were in readiness to follow him in an unauthorized military expedition to revolutionize the western United States and separate it from the United States. There he planned to establish a monarchy with him at the head. New Orleans would be the his capital.

When the rumors reached the executives of the Mississippi Territory, the President made a proclamation warning *all good citizens against the unlawful enterprise which was contemplated by certain citizens of the United States against the dominions of the King of Spain and commanded all civil and military officers of every grade and department to be active and vigilant in searching out and bringing to punishment all persons engaged in such enterprise, by all lawful means within their power.*

The whole country was in a state of excitement and apprehension on account of the danger of anarchy and civil war. On the 14th of January, intelligence was received at Natchez that Colonel Burr, with about sixty men had arrived at the mouth of the Bayou Pierre. The acting governor immediately issued orders for activating the miltia and prepare them for marching orders.

Twenty-four hours later, in the evening and under an inclement sky, Colonel Ferdinand L. Claiborne led two hundred and seventy-five on a voyage to the mouth of Cole's Creek, twenty-five miles above Natchez. There the men were joined by a troop of cavalry from Jefferson county. Two of the acting governor's aids, Major Shields and Major Poindexter were sent to Burr's encampment near Bayou Pierre with a message notifying him of the military movements against him and inviting him to surrender himself and the men with him into the hands of the civil authorities.

Colonel Burr agreed to meet Governor Mead the next day at the house of Thomas Calvit who lived near Colonel Claiborne's encampment. His friend, Colonel Fitpatrick of Jefferson County, would also meet with them.

The next day, Colonel Burr traveled to the Claibornes's encampment and was then escorted to the appointed interview with the acting governor, where he agreed to surrender himself, thirteen boats, and sixty men. He proceeded as a prisoner in the company of the governor to Washington in the Mississippi Territory.

Colonel Burr appeared before Judge Rodney of the Superior Court and with his sureties, of Lyman Harding, Esq., and Colonel Benajah Osmun and for a payment of the sum of ten thousand dollars, he entered a plea to be released. Judge Rodney released him from custody and his next court appearance was scheduled for the session on the 3rd of February. His men were also liberated upon parole in Natchez.

On Monday the 3rd of February the extra session of the Superior Court was held in the town of Washington in the Mississippi Territory and Colonel Burr attended with his counsel, William B. Shields and Lyman Harding, Esquires.

After the grand jury delivered the charge, the court was adjourned until the next day. Colonel Burr demanded a dismissal of charges which the court promptly refused. The court session was continued for the following day, but Colonel Burr did not appear in court. It was soon ascertained that he had escaped during the night.

Governor Williams issued a proclamation offering a reward of two thousand dollars for the apprehension and delivery of Aaron Burr, either to him in Washington or to the Federal authorities of the United States. A troop of cavalry was dispatched to Claiborne County in search of the fugitive.

Vice-President Arrested In Alabama

Aaron Burr traveled by night as he began making his way down the Tombigbee River to reach Pensacola in order to obtain the protection of a British vessel in the harbor. Governor Williams strongly suspected he received assistance from sympathetic citizens of the town of Washington. Burr was captured near Fort Stoddart in Washington County, Alabama. The excerpt below from Albert J. Picketts, *History of Alabama*, provides the colorful details of his capture in Alabama.

During a cold night in February, two young men-Nicholas Perkins, a lawyer, and Thomas Malone, clerk of the court were sitting in their cabin, in the village of Wakefield, Washington County, Alabama. Before them was a backgammon board, and they were absorbed in the playing of that game. The hour was ten o'clock. The distant tramp of horses arrested their attention.

Two travellers presently rode up to the door, one of who inquired for the tavern. It was pointed out to him, and then he asked the road to Colonel Hinson's. Perkins informed him that the route lay over difficult paths, the place was seven miles distant, and a dangerous creek intervened. The fire, being replenished with pine, now threw a light in the face of the traveller who propounded these questions.

His countenance appeared to Perkins exceedingly interesting. His eyes sparkled like diamonds, while he sat upon his splendid horse, caparisoned with a fine saddle and new holsters. His dress was that of a plain farmer, but beneath his coarse pantaloons protruded a pair of exquisitely shaped boots.

His striking features with the strange mixture of his apparel, aroused the suspicions of Perkins, and, no sooner had the two travelers ridden from the door, than he said to Malone, with the most earnest gesticulation, "That is Aaron Burr. I have read a description of him in the proclamation. I cannot be mistaken. Let us follow him to Hinson's, and take measures for his arrest."

Malone declined to accompany him, remonstrating, at the same time, upon the folly of pursuing a traveler, at such a late hour of the night, and upon the basis of the merest conjecture. Perkins now rushed to the cabin of Theodore Brightwell, the sheriff, and awoke him. Presently these men were seen riding off with a rapid pace. The night was bitter cold, and the pine trees of the forest sadly moaned.

The travelers strangely made their way to the residence of Hinson, where they arrived about half past eleven o'clock. The moon had just risen, and enabled the lady of the house, whose husband was absent, to see that they were travelers, by their saddle-bags and tin cups, as she timidly peeped through a small window. She made no answer to their "halloo," but quietly closed the window. The strangers alighted and went into the kitchen, where a cheerful fire was yet burning.

Perkins and the sheriff soon came in sight of the house. The former, recollecting that he had already been seen at Wakefield, thought it politic to remain in the woods, until Brightwell could go in the house, make the necessary discoveries, and return to him. Mrs. Hinson was a relative of the sheriff, and, recognizing his voice, felt relieved by his appearance from the fears she had felt in consequence of the strangers having come at such a late hour of the night.

Brightwell repaired to the kitchen and discovered one of these men sitting by the fire, with his head down, while a handkerchief partially concealed his face. His companion had gone to the stable to assist a negro in taking care of the horses. It was not long before they went into the main building, where the hostess had hastily prepared supper. While the elder traveler was eating, he engaged her in a sprightly conversation, in which he often thanked her for her kindness. At the same time he cast the keenest glances at the sheriff, who stood before the fire, evidently with the endeavor to read his thoughts and intentions.

After he had finished his supper, he arose from the table, bowed to the lady, walked back to the kitchen and took his seat by the fire. Mrs. Hinson then turned to his companion, and said, "Have I not, sir, the honor of entertaining Colonel Burr, the gentleman who has just walked out?" He gave her no answer, but rose from the table, much embarrassed, and also repaired to the kitchen. Her question had been prompted by Brightwell.

In the morning, after breakfast, the elder traveler sought an interview with the lady, took occasion again to thank her for the hospitable attentions, regretted the absence of her husband, inquired the route to Pensacola, and rode off with his companion.

Perkins remained at his post in the woods, shivering with cold, and wondering why Brightwell did not return to him. His patience at length became exhausted, and, believing the person he was pursuing to be really Burr, he mounted his horse, and rode rapidly to the house of Joseph Bates, Sr., at Nannahubba Bluff.

Procuring from that gentleman a negro and a canoe, he paddled down the river, and arrived at Fort Stoddart at the breaking of day. Rushing into the fort, and acquainting Captain Edward P. Gaines with his suspicions, the latter made instant preparations to take the road.

After a hasty breakfast, about the rising of the sun, Gaines, placing himself at the head of a file of mounted soldiers, rode off with Perkins.

About nine o'clock that morning they met the two mysterious travelers, on the descent of a hill, near a wolf pen, at the distance of two miles from the residence of Hinson. The following conversation immediately ensued:

GAINES-I presume, sir, I have the honor of addressing Colonel Burr.

STRANGER-I'm a traveler in the country, and do not recognize your right to ask such a question.

GAINES-I arrest you at the instance of the Federal Government.

STRANGER-By what authority do you arrest a traveler upon the highway, on his own private business?

GAINES-I am an officer of the army. I hold in my hands the proclamations of the President and the Governor, directing your arrest.

STRANGER—You are a young man, and may not be aware of the responsibilities which result from arresting travelers.

GAINES-I am aware of the responsibilities, but I know my duty.

The stranger now became exceedingly animated, and with much eloquence and force denounced these proclamations as documents which had emanated in malevolent feeling, without any just foundation, and endeavored again to frighten the young officer from discharging his duty, by ingeniously adverting upon the great liabilities which he was about to assume.

But Gaines sternly replied, "My mind is made up. You must accompany me to Fort Stoddart, where you shall be treated with all the respect due the ex-Vice-president of the United States, so long as you make no attempt to escape from me."

The stranger for a moment gazed at him with earnestness, apparently surprised at the unusual firmness which the young officer exhibited. He then assented, by a gentle motion of his head, wheeled his horse around, and took the road to the fort, riding by the side of the captain. His traveling companion rode back toward Wakefield with Brightwell, the sheriff who was in company with the two travelers when they were met by Gaines.[2]

The party reached the fort in the evening, and Colonel Burr, being

---

2   It remains a mystery to this day why Brightwell did not keep his promise with Perkins, and I can only account for it by supposing that he became fascinated with Colonel Burr, was sorry that he had sought to arrest him, and was now conducting him to Mrs. Carson's ferry, upon the Tombigby, on the route to Pensacola. Burr had seen Colonel Hinson at Natchez, who had invited him to his house should he ever pass that way. When he escaped from Natchez he was secreted, from time to time, at the houses of his friends, and he was hastening to Hinson's with whom he had intended to pass a week. But when he found him absent, and himself discovered by Brightwell, who probably informed him of the intentions of Perkins, he determined to fly to Pensacola, and there take a ship for Europe. He intended to enlist wealthy and influential persons, both in England and France, in the scheme of making the conquest of the North American Spanish posessions, now that he had so signally failed to accomplish it in the United States.

conducted to his room, took his dinner alone. Late in the night, he heard a groan in an adjoining room. He arose from a table, at which he was reading, opened the door, entered the room, and approached the bedside of Geo. S. Gaines, the brother of the commandant, who was sick. He was kind to the sufferer, felt of his pulse, said he had traveled much and knew something of medicine, and offered his services. They now entered into an agreeable conversation. Burr asked the Choctaw factor many questions about the Indians and their commerce.

The next day he appeared at the dinner table, and was introduced to the wife of the commandant, who was the daughter of Judge Harry Toulmin. In the evening, he played chess with that accomplished lady, and, during his confinement at the fort, was often her competitor in that intricate game.

Every night he sought the company of the invalid, who became exceedingly attached to him, and who felt deep regret on account of the downfall of so interesting and so distinguished a character. Often did the good heart of George S. Gaines grieve over the adversities and trials of this remarkable man, as they discoursed together. In all their conversations, maintained every night, the impenetrable Burr never once alluded to the designs which he had failed to carry out, to his present arrest, or to his future plans.

In the meantime, Captain Gaines had been untiring in his exertions to fit out an expedition for the conveyance of his distinguished prisoner to the federal city. At length he placed Burr in a boat, along with a file of soldiers, and he was rowed up the Alabama river and then into Lake Tensaw.

Passing some houses on the banks, several ladies wept upon seeing the ex-Vice-President a prisoner, and one of them named a son for him. Everywhere in the Southwest the ladies were attached to the man, and suffered their feelings to become enlisted in behalf of his unfortunate enterprises. It is a prominent and noble trait in the female character to admire a man of daring and generous impulses and to pity and defend him in his adversities![3]

---

3   Burr was not only popular with the ladies, but the most prominent men in

Arriving at the Boat Yard, Burr disembarked and was delivered to the guard which was so long to be with him in dangers and fatigues. It consisted of Colonel Nicholas Perkins, of Tennessee, who had, as we have seen, been the cause of his arrest, Thomas Malone, formerly a clerk in the land office at Raleigh, North Carolina, but who, was a clerk of the court of Washington county, Alabama, Henry B. Slade, of North Carolina, John Mills, a native of Alabama, John Henry, of Tennessee, two brothers, named McCormack, of Kentucky, and two federal soldiers.

With the exception of the two soldiers, Perkins had chosen these men on account of the confidence which he reposed in their honor, energy and fidelity. He had been placed over them by Captain Gaines, who entertained a high opinion of his bravery and capacity.

Perkins took his men aside and obtained from them the most solemn pledge that they would not suffer the prisoner to influence them in any manner in his behalf; to avoid which, they promised to converse as little as possible with him upon the whole route to Washington. The character of Burr for making strong impressions in his favor upon the human mind was well known to Perkins.

When the prisoner fled from the Natchez settlements he assumed a disguised dress. He was still attired in it. It consisted of coarse pantaloons, made of homespun of a copperas dye, and a roundabout of inferior drab cloth, while his hat was a flapping, wide-brimmed beaver, which had in times past been white, but now presented a variety of dingy colors.

When the guard was ready to depart he mounted the same elegant horse which he rode when arrested. He bestrode him most gracefully, flashed his large dark eyes upon the many bystanders, audibly bade them farewell, and departed.[4] Perkins and his men were well provided with large pistols, which they carried in holsters, while the two soldiers had

---

the Southwest favored his enterprise, as they had long been anxious for the expulsion of the Spaniards.

4 Many persons who saw Burr in Alabama have told us that his eyes were peculiarly brilliant, and, to use the comparison of Malone," they looked like stars."

muskets.

They left the Boat Yard, a quarter of a mile from which the terrible massacre of Fort Mims afterwards occurred, and, pursuing the Indian path, encamped the first night in the lower part of the present county of Monroe.

The only tent taken along was pitched for Burr, and under it he lay the first night by large fires, which threw a glare over the dismal woods. All night his ears were saluted with the fierce and disagreeable howling of wolves.

In the wilds of Alabama, in a small tent, reposed this remarkable man, surrounded by a guard, and without a solitary friend or congenial spirit. He was a prisoner of the United States, for whose liberties he had fought; and an exile from New York, whose statutes and institutions bore the impress of his mind.

Death had deprived him of his accomplished wife, his only child was on the distant coast of Carolina, his professional pursuits were abandoned, his fortune swept from him, the magnificent scheme of the conquest of Mexico defeated, and he was harassed from one end of the Union to the other. All these things were sufficient to weigh down an ordinary being and hurry him to the grave. Burr, however, was no common man. In the morning he rose with a cheerful face, and fell into traveling order, along with the taciturn and watchful persons who had charge of him.

Although guarded with vigilance, he was treated with respect and kindness, and his few wants were gratified. The trail, like all Indian highways, was narrow, which required the guard to march in single file, with Burr in the middle of the line. The route lay about eight miles south of the present city of Montgomery, then an Indian town called Econchate.

Passing by the residence of "Old Milly," who, as we have seen, lived upon the creek in Montgomery county, which still bears her name, Perkins employed her husband, a mulatto named Evans, to conduct the guard across Line Creek, Cubahatchee and Calabee, all of which they were forced to swim.

It was a perilous and fatiguing march, and for days the rain descended in chilling torrents upon these unsheltered horsemen, collecting in deep and rapid rivulets at every point.

Hundreds of Indians, too, thronged the trail, and the party might have been killed in one moment. But the fearless Perkins bore on his distinguished prisoner, amid angry elements and human foes.

In the journey through Alabama the guard always slept in the woods, near swamps of reed, upon which the belled and hobbled horses fed during the night. After breakfast, it was their custom again to mount their horses and march on, with a silence which was sometimes broken by a remark about the weather, the creeks or the Indians.

Burr sat firmly in the saddle, was always on the alert, and was a most excellent rider. Although drenched for hours with cold and clammy rain, and at night extended upon a thin pallet, on the bare ground, after having accomplished a ride of forty miles each day, yet, in the whole distance to Richmond, this remarkable man was never heard to complain that he was sick, or even fatigued.

At the Chattahoochee was a crossing place, owned by an Indian named Marshall, where the effects of the expedition were carried over the river in canoes, by the sides of which the horses swam. In this manner they passed the Flint and Ockmulgee.

Arriving at Fort Wilkinson, on the Oconee, Perkins entered the first ferry-boat which he had seen upon the whole route, and, a few miles beyond the river, was sheltered by the first roof, a house of entertainment, kept by one Bevin.

While breakfast was in a state of preparation, and the guard were quietly sitting before a large fire, the publican began a series of questions; and learning that the party were from the "Bigby settlement," he immediately fell upon the fruitful theme of Aaron Burr, the traitor.

He asked if he had not been arrested, if he was not a very bad man and if every one was not afraid of him. Perkins and the rest of the guard, much annoyed and embarrassed, hung down their heads, and made no reply.

Burr, who was sitting in a corner near the fire, majestically raised his head, and flashing his fiery eye upon Bevin, said: "I am Aaron Burr; what is it you want with me?"

Struck with the keenness of his look, the solemnity of his voice, and the dignity of his manner, Bevin stood aghast, and trembled like a leaf. He asked not another question of the guard, but quietly moved about the house, offering the most obsequious attentions.

When Perkins reached the confines of South Carolina, he watched the prisoner more closely than ever, for in this State lived Colonel Joseph Alston, a, man of talents and influence, afterwards governor-who had married the only daughter, and, indeed, the only child of Burr.

Afraid that the prisoner would be rescued at some point in this State, he exhorted his men to renewed vigilance. Before entering the town, in which is situated the Court House of Chester District, South Carolina, he made a halt, and placed two men in front of Burr, two behind, and two on either side of him.

In this manner they passed near a tavern, at the Court House, where many persons were standing in front of the portico, while music and dancing were heard in the house. Seeing the collection of men so near him, Burr threw himself from his horse, and exclaimed in a loud voice, "I AM AARON BURR, UNDER MILITARY ARREST, AND CLAIM THE PROTECTION OF THE CIVIL AUTHORITIES."

Perkins, with several of the guard, immediately dismounted, and the former ordered the prisoner to remount. Burr, in a most defiant manner, said, "I WILL NOT!"

Being unwilling to shoot him, Perkins threw down his pistols, both of which he held in his hands, and seizing Burr around the waist with the grasp of a tiger, threw him into his saddle. Thomas Malone caught the reins of the prisoner's horse, slipped them over his head, and led the animal rapidly on, while others whipped him up from behind.

The astonished citizens saw a party enter their village with a prisoner, heard him appeal to them for protection in the most imploring manner, saw armed men immediately surround him and thrust him again into his saddle, and then the whole party vanish from their presence, before they could recover from their confusion. The least timidity or hesitation on the part of Perkins would have lost him his prisoner, for the latter was still popular in South Carolina.

Far in the outskirts of the town the party halted. Burr was in a high state of excitement, and burst into a flood of tears.

The kind-hearted Malone also wept, at seeing the low condition to which this conspicuous man was now reduced. The bold attempt to escape, and the irresolution of the people to whom he appealed, suddenly unmanned him. Perkins held a short consultation with some of his men, and sending Burr on the route in charge of the guard, with Malone in command, he went back to the village, and purchasing a gig overtook the party before night. Burr was placed in this vehicle and driven by Malone, escorted by the guard.

Without further incident they arrived at Fredericksburg, where dispatches from Jefferson caused them to take Burr to Richmond. The ladies of the latter place vied with each other in contributing to the comforts of the distinguished ex-Vice-president, yielding him fruit, wine, and a variety of fine apparel. Perkins and his men repaired to Washington, reported to the President, and returned to Alabama by the distant route of Tennessee.

Aaron Burr was arraigned for treason, and was tried and acquitted. He was then arraigned for misdemeanor, and was tried and acquitted. Thus ended the most expensive and extraordinary trial known to the country. A part of the time that he was in Richmond the Federal Government caused him to be confined in the upper story of the penitentiary, where he was permitted to enjoy the company of his daughter.

Sailing to Europe, Burr was at first treated with great distinction in England. The winter of 1809 found him in Edinburgh. Residing some time in Sweden and Germany, he at length arrived in France, where Bonaparte, influenced by letters from America, conceived a prejudice against him so immovable that he refused him passports to leave the country.

At length the Duke de Bassano procured him the necessary documents, when he sailed for America, and arrived at New York on the 8th of June, 1812. Here he engaged again in the lucrative practice of the law, living in dignified obscurity, if such a position could be assigned to a man of his notoriety. He died at Staten Island, on the 11th of September, 1836, at the advanced age of eighty. His body, attended by his relations and friends, was taken to Princeton, New Jersey, and interred among the graves of his ancestors.

The following comments are also by Albert J. Pickett.

With the private character of Burr, we conceive we have nothing to do, except to add that we believe him to have been n most profligate and licentious man.

When the world put him down-when he received nothing but abuse and ingratitude from those who once sycophantically surrounded him, and whom he had helped to offices of honor and profit-when he was shunned by his old companions in arms, not invited into the society of the refined, but was pointed at, in walking Broadway, as the murderer and the traitor--he became disheartened and soured; and, being without those religious feelings which sustain the most unfortunate, he threw off every restraint, and gave a loose rein to sentiments always unprincipled, and to passions always strong.[5]

---

[5] In relation to Burr's arrest in Alabama, and his journey through the wilderness, I conversed with Mr. Thomas Malone, one of his guard; with Mrs. Hinson,

One of the gravest facts proved against Burr, at his trial at Richmond, upon the evidence of General Wilkinson, was that the prisoner, in a letter written to him in cipher, he avowed his design of seizing upon Baton Rouge, as a preliminary measure, and, afterwards, extending his conquests into the Spanish provinces.

Burr Trial (Library of Congress)

Admitting this to be true, it did not prove that he intended to dismember the Union. Our readers have already seen that the Federal Government, and the people of the Southwest, desired the expulsion of the Spaniards from the Baton Rouge district, which was a part of the purchase from Napoleon, when he sold us Louisiana; and hereafter, it will be seen that these Spaniards were driven from the Baton Rouge district only three years after Burr's trial, when the governor of it, Colonel Grandpre, was killed.

---

now Mrs. Sturdevant, at whose house Burr passed the night when he was discovered, with Mr. George S. Gaines. who was at Fort Stoddart when he was brought there; and with Mrs. Howse, who saw him when they were conducting him up Lake Tensaw. I also corresponded with Major-General Gaines, and have his testimony. All these witnesses are reputable, and as respectable as any persons in Alabama. On the subject of Burr's early life, and of his operations in the Western country, I consulted Memoirs of Aaron Burr, by M. L. Davis, the various American State Papers, Clarke's Proofs of the Corruption of Wilkinson; Memoirs of Wilkinson, by himself; Familiar Letters upon Public Characters, and many other work

In the citizens of the Southwest, who accomplished this end, it was not held to be treason, but Burr, for merely contemplating it, was tried for that crime.

It was not considered treason, when President Jackson allowed hundreds of people of the Southwest to be shipped from Mobile and New Orleans, with arms in their hands, who presently landed upon the coast of Texas, and took that country from the Spaniards. But, for similar designs, Aaron Burr was hunted down, thrown into prison, and tried for treason.

The impartial reader must arrive at the conclusion that the faults of Burr, in a political and public capacity, were not such as ought really to have placed that odium upon him which still attaches to his name.

One of the great secrets of his political misfortunes lay in the prejudices and malevolence of politicians and fanatics.

Somebody heard General Washington say that Burr was a dangerous man; " thereupon the world set him down as a dangerous man." He killed Hamilton in a duel, because Hamilton abused him; thereupon the world said he was a murderer."

He was a formidable rival of Jefferson in the contest for the Presidency; thereupon a majority of the republican party said he was a political scoundrel. He had always opposed the federal party; for that reason the federal party hated him with exceeding bitterness.

A blundering, extravagant man, named Herman Blannerhassett, sought Burr while he was in the West, eagerly enlisted in his schemes, and invited him to his house; thereupon William Wirt said, in his prosecuting speech, that Burr was the serpent who entered the garden of Eden."

We do not wish to be considered as the defender of Aaron Burr. We do not admire his character, or that of many of his distinguished contemporaries who assailed him. But, as a historian, we are expected to write the truth, even if that truth is unpalatable to the prejudices of the age.

Hero Of The Alamo Kills An Alabama Man

Colonel William Barrett Travis, hero of the Alamo was born in Edgefield District, South Carolina, (near Old Fort Ninety -Six,) on August 9, 1809. He was the son of Mark Travis, Sr. and Jemima Stallworth, early pioneers to Conecuh County, Alabama.

Painting of Col. William Barrett Travis died 1836 at Alamo

Mark and Jemima (Stallworth) Travis were married Jan 1, 1808 in South Carolina. They moved to Conecuh County, Alabama in 1815 and were among the earliest pioneers of Conecuh County. William Barrett Travis was the oldest of eleven children.

Travis was educated in the small schools in the rough frontier of

Alabama and then later at an academy in Sparta. Finally, his uncle Reverend Alexander Travis, a renowned Baptist minister, enrolled him in an academy at Claiborne, Alabama. When he reached the age of maturity, he studied for the bar in Claiborne under the leading attorney Hon. James Dellett. He later became a partner with Dellett for a brief time.

William Barrett Travis married Rosanna Cato on Oct 26, 1828 and they had their first son Charles Edward Travis, born August 8, 1829. He began publishing a newspaper, the Claiborne Herald, was a member of Alabama Masonic Lodge No. 3. and in the 26th Alabama Militia.

There is a rumor that in 1831, after returning from a business trip William Barrett Travis discovered his wife had been unfaithful. Of course, actual evidence is lacking but the story persists that he killed the man implicated with his wife, renounced the paternity of his yet unborn child Susanna Isabella and left for Texas, abandoning his family. Rosanna and William Barrett Travis were divorced January 9, 1836 and Rosanna married Samuel Grandin Cloud Feb. 14, 1836.

William Barrett Travis became a lawyer in Texas and was one of the first to join the Texas force when friction developed between Mexico and Texas. On orders from the Provisional Governor in January of 1836, Travis entered the Alamo with about 30 men and commanded the Texas defenders during the Siege and Battle of the Alamo. His appeal for reinforcements has become an American symbol of unyielding courage and heroism. Although a few reinforcements arrived before the Alamo fell, Col. Travis and over 180 defenders gave their lives for Texas independence on 6 March 1836.

In his last message out he stated "Take care of my little boy. If the country should be saved, I may make him a splendid fortune; but if the country should be lost, and I should perish, he will have nothing but the proud recollection that he is the son of a man who died for his country." Travis was only twenty-six years of age at the time of his death.

His son, Charles Edward Travis was living with his married sister Susan Isabella (Travis) Grissett in the 1850 census of Monroe County, Alabama and had the occupation of a teacher. Susan Isabella had two children

William Barrett Grissett and Mary Jane Grissett.

Charles Edward Travis won a seat in the Texas Legislature in 1853. The brother and sister were still together in Chapel Hill, Washington County, Texas in 1860 census. Charles Edward Travis was single, and a lawyer with considerable property. He had obtained a law degree from Baylor University in 1859, but died within a year of consumption.

Susan's husband John D. Grissett also had a good deal of property in the 1860 census. Only Mary Jane, their daughter was listed, their son William Barrett Grissett died in 1855. Though William Barrett Travis questioned the paternity of Susan Isabella, he still named her in his will.

Fear Of War With The Native Americans Looms Ahead

Man Killed By Indians – War Threat

About the year 1800 a brisk migration had begun from Georgia and the Carolinas, through the Creek country, to the Mississippi Territory. Samuel Dale, then a Georgian, placed three wagons and teams on this route of migration, transporting families westward and taking back to Savannah loads of Native American produce. In 1803 a road was marked out through the Cherokee nation.

Within the area where Washington and Clarke county now exist, many enterprising settlers built their cabins and began to establish their homes.

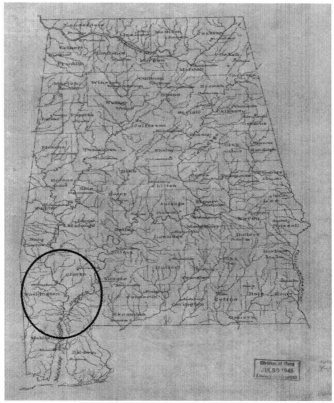

1893 Map of Alabama with Clarke & Washington Counties circled (Library of Congress)

These river settlements at the time were completely isolated. On the south were the Spaniards, on the east were the Creeks, on the west, between them and the Natchez and Yazoo settlements, were the Choctaws, and on the north the nearest settlement was in the bend of the Tennessee.

By an act of Congress on May 14, 1812, the territory lying east of the Pearl river, west of Perdido, and south of the thirty-first degree of latitude, was annexed to the Mississippi territory. The Spaniards however did not entirely give this territory up until forced to do so in 1813.

In 1812, Samuel Dale moved Colonel J. Phillips and family to Point Jackson on the Tombigbee River and started his teams back to Georgia. On his return trip to Georgia he traveled to Pensacola which was the place of trade for Indians and white settlers.

In Pensacola, Dale heard from a "half-breed Creek, called Sam Manac, that the Creeks were getting arms from the Spaniards at Pensacola and that when the Indians on the Coosa, Tallapoosa, and Black Warrior were sufficiently furnished with guns, powder and lead, they planned to attack the settlement in the forks of the Tombigbee and Alabama." (Dale) As he returned to the Georgia trail, he met a party of men who had just buried a man named Daly who had been murdered by the Indians. They encouraged him to return with them to the settlements on the Tombigbee, but he wouldn't.

In his own words, he stated the following about his experience.

My business, however, compelled me to proceed, and I concluded to lay by during the day and travel by night. About midnight, near the forks of the Wolf-path—a noted trail in those days—I perceived a light, and at the same moment a dog gave the alarm.

It was very dark, but, distinctly hearing footsteps approaching, I rode off some forty steps and dismounted, placing my horse between me and the Indians in the event of their firing, and at the same time transferring from my saddle-bags to my person a pocket-book containing eight hundred dollars, resolved to save my life and money too, if I could.

They advanced within thirty paces, and paused; but, hearing no sound, one cried out, 'He has gone back,' and they went rapidly on the path I traveled. Fortunately, it was too dark to note the footprints of my horse, and to this circumstance, under Providence, I owe my life.

As soon as they were out of ear-shot I pushed cautiously forward, and got to Samuel Manac's, a friendly half-breed, on Catoma Creek, about daybreak. He informed me that the road was beset, and that it would be difficult to get through.

The Shawnee poison had already begun to work. The hostile portion of the Indians were in arms in small parties, murdering friendly Indians and whites. I concealed myself that day, but traveled all night, and about daybreak lighted at Bob Mosely's stand, which stood at the edge of Peter McQueen's town. McQueen was a half-blood, of property and influence, shrewd, sanguinary, and deceitful, and had already declared for war.

Mosely's wife—a most excellent, kind - hearted woman, niece of McQueen —soon brought me a cup of coffee, and contriving to dispatch two Indian lads, who were present, on some errand, she whispered to me that her uncle was going to war on the white people, and had sworn that he would kill me on sight for bringing so many settlers into the country. The very party I had just escaped he had sent to watch the path for me.

I immediately took to the woods, hiding during the day and traveling by night. On one occasion I took the wrong trail, and rode plump up to a band of hostiles at We-tum-kee; but they were so absorbed in a war-dance I got off without being discovered. I finally reached McIntosh's in safety, and dispatched a runner to Colonel Hawkins with the news; but he was even then firmly persuaded that the hostilities of the Creeks would only be directed against each other—that it was a war of factions, headed by McQueen on one side and the Big Warrior on the other, and would not be directed against the whites. He appreciated the many noble traits of the Indians, but never understood their perfidy in war, nor the skill with which they can disguise their intentions.

My next enterprise was to move Judge Saffold and family to the Tombigbee in June, 1813. I knew that a detachment of troops had been ordered from Fort Mitchell to Mobile, and my plan was to obtain their convoy. When our party reached the fort the detachment was two days in advance; but we pushed on in their wake, and I had the satisfaction of lodging the judge and his estimable family safely at their new home.

On this journey I saw enough to satisfy me that the Indians had determined on war. Sam Manac, a noted half-breed of the nation, made to me and John E. Myles the following statement on the 13th of July, 1813, which I forwarded to Colonel James Caller, commanding the 15th regiment of militia, Mississippi Territory.

MANAC'S STATEMENT

About the last of October thirty northern Indians came with Tecumseh, who said he had been sent by his brother the Prophet, the servant of the Great Spirit. They attended our great council at Took-a-batcha. I was there three days, but every day he refused to deliver his talk, saying that 'the sun had traveled too far.' The day after I left the ground he delivered it.

It was not until about December following that our people began to dance the war-dance. It has been the practice of the Muscogees to dance after war, not before. In December about forty of our warriors begun this northern custom, and my brother-in-law, Francis, who pretends to be a prophet, at the head of them; now, more than half of the Creek nation engage in this dance.

I drove some steers to Pensacola not long since, and during my absence my brother-in-law and sister, who have joined the war party, came to my plantation, and carried away my best horses and cattle, and thirty-six negroes.

A few days since I fell in with a party from the Autassee towns on the Tallapoosa, led by High-head Jim, bound for Pensacola for ammunition. He came up, shook me by the hand, and immediately began to tremble and jerk in every part of his body. Even the muscles of his face and the calves of his legs were convulsed, and his whole frame seemed to be drawn up and knotted by spasms.

This practice was first taught to Francis by a Shawnee prophet, and began to be practiced by the war party in May last. High-head Jim asked me what I meant to do. In apprehension of my life, I answered, 'I will sell my property and join you.'

He then said they were bound for Pensacola with a letter from a British general to the Spanish governor, which would enable them to get all the arms they needed; that this letter had been given to the Little Warrior when he was in Canada last year, and when he was killed it was sent to the prophet Francis.

He said that, after getting what was wanted from Pensacola, the Indians on the Coosa, Tallapoosa, and Black Warrior would attack the settlements in the forks of Tombigbee and Alabama; that the Cherokees would attack the Tennesseeans, the Seminoles the Georgians, and the Choctaws the settlements on the Mississippi.

He said, likewise, that the war party had resolved to kill the Big Warrior, Alexander and James Curnell, Captain Isaacs, William McIntosh, the Mad Dragoon's son, the Little Prince, Spoko-Kangee, Tallasee-Thic-si-co, and others who had listened to the talk of the whites. High-head Jim said that Peter McQueen, when all the parties for Pensacola got together, would have three hundred warriors, and on his return would destroy the Tensaw settlements.

Every Free White Male – 16 to 50 Was Subject To Serve In the Militia

With worries of future difficulties and to maintain order within the new settlements, a militia was essential in early Alabama. The first plan to organize the militia within the Mississippi Territory was the Militia Law of 1807.

Under this law every free while male citizen from sixteen to fifty years of age was subject to enrollment. Exceptions were only made for territorial officers—judicial and executive, licensed ministers of the gospel, keepers of the public jails, and keepers of public ferries.

The law stated the following:

That every citizen so enrolled and notified, shall, within six months thereafter, or as soon as such can be had in the territory, provide himself with a good musquet (sic) or fire-lock, a sufficient bayonet and belt, two spare flints and a knap-sack, a pouch, with a box to contain therein not less than twenty- four cartridges, suited to the bore of his musquet or fire-lock, to contain a proper quantity of powder and ball; or with a good rifle, knapsack, shot-pouch and powder-horn, twenty balls suited to the bore of his rifle, and a quarter of a pound of powde ; and shall appear so armed, accoutred and provided, when called out, to exercise, or into service, except when called out on company days to exercise only, when he may appear without a knapsack. The commissioned officers severally shall be armed with a sword or hanger...,

The general plan of organization was based upon one regiment of two battalions in each county, which was to consist of as many companies of forty-five members, rank and file, as could be formed with the whole comprising one brigade. The officers included a brigadier-general, with one brigade inspector who served also as brigade major; and for each regiment, a lieutenant, colonel commandant; for each battalion, a major; for each company, a captain, a lieutenant, an ensign, four sergeants, four corporals, a drummer, a fifer or bugler; the non-commissioned officers to be appointed by the captain.

The regimental staff officers were: an adjutant, a quartermaster, a paymaster, a surgeon and a surgeon's mate, a sergeant major, a drum major, and a fife major, all appointed by the commanding officer.

At the outset a muster of every company was required to be held every three months; a battalion muster in February, and a regimental muster in October of each year.

The Governor was empowered to call out such number of militia troops as he might think necessary to quell insurrection or repel invasion, and while in active service they were governed by the United States articles of war and received the same pay and rations as United States troops.

The organization also provided for a "patrol" to regulate and discipline roving or unruly slaves and other disorderly persons, and a system of fines and forfeitures to insure enrollment and attendance at musters and drills. The administration of the disciplinary system was in the hands of courts martial composed of designated militia officers.

Margaret Eades – Witness To Indian Wars

Margaret Eades was the wife of Jeremiah Austill an early pioneer of Alabama. She witnessed many of the bloody scenes of the Creek Indian War of 1813-14 and describes the initial days of the outbreak in the excerpt below.

Note: *This has been transcribed exactly as written, with some words misspelled.*

Part I

One night our sentinels were hailed by Jere Austill, they came and awoke Father, who went out immediately and let him in. He told Father that the Fort Sinquefield had stampeded, the people all making for our Fort or St. Stephens, and the people in his Father's Fort, near Suggsville, were in the act of breaking up too, but they had concluded to send him down to the arsenal for a Company of Regulars, and if they could get them, they would hold the Fort.

Mother roused the cook, and gave Jere a nice supper at midnight, Father put him over the river and saw the General, told his business, and was glad to hear the order for the Company to come back with him, but Jere begged to be excused, said "Send the soldiers, but I must travel alone."

We fared very well in the Fort, thanks to Hannah, the faithful servant that stayed at home. She made the garden, milked the cows, churned the butter, raised chickens, and came every other day to the Fort with a large basket on her head. Mother would say, "Hannah, you are a jewel, what would we do without you, thanks to your blue eyes." So often she said she saw moccasin tracks in the path.

Time passed on with fear and trembling with the grown folks, but we children engaged every moment. I was in every tent in the day, some laughable things would occur. There was a Mrs. Smith, quite an original, she was a very good woman, but violent tempered. The boys took great delight in teasing her, she often threw hot water on them, one day the carpenters were at work building a block house to mount a cannon on the top, two of the men became outrageously mad with each other, and Garner, a great bully, who was always kicking up a fuss, drew a broadax on a defenseless man, screaming he would split him open.

The man took to his heels and Garner after him, threw tents over women and children, finally the man ran through Mrs. Smith's, and Garner after him, full tilt, the old lady grabbed up a three-legged stool, saying " --- dead", but I let him have it, one corner of the stool struck Garner on the temple, and down he went, blood spurting from his nose. She thought she had killed him dead. She ran over to Mother's tent and said, "Where is Captain Eades? By the Lord I have killed Garner, and he must put me over the river, for Garner's folks will string me up if they catch me."

She ran to meet Father, and he took her to the river and set her over in the canebrake. She said, "Now you go back, and if Garner is dead, you come to the bluff and whistle on your thumbs, then by the Lord Old Betsy Smith is off to the Choctaw Nation." When Father returned, Garner had been brought around, and after that became a very quiet and peaceful man, never bragged or bullied more during the war.

Part II

After we had been in the Fort six months, the Indians became very hostile, crossed the Alabama and burned houses, corn, destroyed cattle, and killed people that were at home in spite of all that could be done by the scouts. Every family was obliged to go into a Fort.

There was an old widow named Cobb, who had two sons old enough to be in the service, but she told them to stay at home and make corn, she was not afraid of Indians, but one day while the boys were plowing in the field, they saw Indians jumping over the fence, the boys stripped the gear off the horses, mounted in a moment, and flew to the house, calling their Mother.

She ran out to meet them, and just as she passed her chimney corner, she saw her dye tub with indigo blue, she just turned the whole contents into her lap, jumped up behind her son and galloped to our Fort from Choctaw Bluff, eight miles. When they arrive, they were all blue, from head to foot. That was the only thing they saved was the thread that was in the blue dye. The women in the Fort all joined and soon made a piece of cloth of the blue, for all had spinning wheels and looms in the Fort, for it was the only way that clothes were obtained in those days.

The day Fort Mims fell was a sad day to all the country. Every heart nearby became paralyzed with fear, and our men that had been so brave, became panic striken, and their families pleading to be taken to Fort St. Stephens.

Father and dear old, Captain Foster spoke to them in vain, they stampeded, some families took to the canebrakes, some to St. Stephens, some down the river to Fort Stoddard where the arsenal is now.

Just as Father and Mother, with Sister and myself were in the act of getting into the canoe to cross the Bigbee, for not a soul was left in the Fort, a young man came running down the bluff calling to Father not to leave him, for God's sake, to be murdered, for the Indians were coming. "Oh, don't leave me, I shall die if you do."

Mother was standing on the bank until we were safely seated, for the canoe was a small one, could only carry four persons. Father told the man that it was impossible for him to take him in that his family must be saved first.

The poor fellow cried out, "Oh, God, I shall be killed." Mother said, "Oh, dear husband, take the coward in, I will wait here until you come after me," and she actually pushed him in, and with her foot sent the canoe flying off, and sat down on the sand quietly waiting Father's return. As soon as the boat struck shore, the fellow made tracks for the Choctaw Nation.

In a few days, after the excitement, all the people returned and pledged themselves to remain and hold the Fort. In the meantime, the young folks were courting and making love, although they were in a Fort expecting to lose their scalps at any moment.

Mr. George S. Gullet became engaged to my sister, Mary Eades, and then implored our parents to allow the marriage, because he could be of so much help to us, could take care of Sister, and then Father would only have Mother and me to take care of, so they consented that the marriage should take place in the Fort.

Mother sent Hannah word that she must get up a large wedding supper, and manage to get it to the Fort. Hannah came down in a complete upsetment, "Name of de Lord, Missus, what I gwine do for all de silibubs and tings for Miss Mary's wedding?"

Mother said, "Never mind, Hannah, make plenty chicken pies, I can buy turkey from the Choctaws, save cream, make plenty of potato custards and huckleberry tarts. We will have coffee enough for all the Fort, so go right at the work." "Well, well, did I ever tink to see de day, did I ebber, my Lord, Miss Mary must be crazy."

But she set to work with a will. Invitations were general to the whole inhabitants of the Fort, they were married, and a jolly wedding it was. One old man sat down to the long table, looked over at Mother, and she said, "Help your self, sir." I thank you, Madam, I will with presumption." I laughed, and being a little girl, was sent off from the table.

Not long after the wedding we had a respite, the Indians were driven back, and all returned joyfully to their houses. Very few had been destroyed this side of Choctaw Bluff, but we could hear of fearful murders. Men would venture too far, and again and again we were forced to return to the Fort until at last General Jackson came to our rescue and finished the war. All the gallant young men joined his army.

My Father carried his provisions up the Alabama in his barge, even as high as Fort Jackson above Wetumpka. Sam Dale, Jere Austill, and many others were with Jackson fighting like heroes for many months, and after the Indians gave up, they went with Jackson to Pensacola and Mobile, some went to New Orleans. Austill was very sick at the Battle pf New Orleans, but one of his cousins was killed there, he was a Files.

About the last of Fourteen all the people were gay, money was plenty, and the people were pouring in by thousands. The County was filled with young men looking for land, school teachers getting up schools. The largest school in the territory was at St. Stephens, there I was sent with many a poor little waif to learn grammar. Our teacher was Mr. Mayhew, from North Carolina, a splendid teacher and good man.

Tecumseh Arrives - Described By A Witness

The Shawnee chief, Tecumseh, came among the Native Americans in the south to incite them to hostilities against the whites. He was the emissary of the British, with whom the federal government was at war. The Spaniards at Pensacola and Mobile had already bred ill-feeling among them against the whites, and the fiery eloquence of Tecumseh precipitated the conflict of the Creek-Indian War.

In 1811, General Samuel Dale attended a grand council of the Creek Indians when Tecumseh appeared. He describes the event and even records Tecumseh's speech in the excerpt below from, *Life and Times of Gen. Sam Dale: The Mississippi Partisan,* Harper & Brothers, 1860.

In 1808, the State of Georgia distributed by lottery a large body of land acquired from the Creek Indians. I drew an excellent water-power, the Flat Shoals, on Commissioner's Creek, and erected a set of mills; but the calling was not to my liking, and I disposed of them, and opened a farm in Jones County, which was for several years my home.

In October, 1811, the annual grand council of the Creek Indians assembled at Tooka-batcha, a very ancient town on the Tallapoosa River. At those annual assemblies the United States Agent for .the Creeks always attended, besides many white and halfbreed traders, and strangers from other tribes.

I accompanied Colonel Hawkins, the United States Agent. A flying rumor had circulated far and near that some of the Northwestern Indians would be present, and this brought some five thousand people to Took-a-batcha, including many Cherokees and Choctaws.

The day after the council met, Tecumseh[6], with a suite of twenty-four

---
6 At the battle of the Holy Ground, which occurred some time after, the prophets left by Tecumseh predicted that the earth would yawn and swallow up General Claiborne and his troops. Tecumseh refers to the Kings of England and Spain,

warriors, marched into the centre of the square, and stood still and erect as so many statues. They were dressed in tanned buckskin huntingshirt and leggins, fitting closely, so as to exhibit their muscular development, and they wore a profusion of silver ornaments; their faces were painted red and black. Each warrior carried a rifle, tomahawk, and war-club. They were the most athletic body of men I ever saw. The famous Jim Bluejacket was among them.

Engraving of Tecumseh ca. 1860 (Library of Congress)

Tecumseh was about six feet high, well put together, not so stout as some of his followers, but of an austere countenance and imperial men. He was in the prime of life.

The Shawnees made no salutation, but stood facing the council-house, not looking to the right or the left. Throughout the assembly there was a

---

who supplied the Indians with arms at Detroit and at Pensacola. The British officers had informed him that a comet would soon appear, and the earthquakes of 1811 had commenced as he came through Kentucky. Like a consummate orator, he refers to them in his speech. When the comet soon after appeared, and the earth began to tremble, they attributed to him supernatural powers, and immediately took up arms.

dead silence.

At length the Big Warrior, a noted chief of the Creeks and a man of colossal proportions, slowly approached, and handed his pipe to Tecumseh. It was passed in succession to each of his warriors; and then the Big Warrior—not a word being spoken— pointed to a large cabin, a few hundred yards from the square, which had previously been furnished with skins and provisions. Tecumseh and his band, in single file, marched to it.

At night they danced, in the style peculiar to the northern tribes, in front of this cabin, and the Creeks crowded around, but no salutations were exchanged. Every morning the chief sent an interpreter to the council-house to announce that he would appear and deliver his talk, but before the council broke up another message came that "the sun had traveled too far, and he would talk next day.

At length Colonel Hawkins became impatient, and ordered his horses to be packed. I told him the Shawnees intended mischief; that I noted much irritation and excitement among the Creeks, and he would do well to remain. He derided my notions, declared that the Creeks were entirely under his control and could not be seduced, that Tecumseh's visit was merely one of show and ceremony, and he laughingly added, "Sam, you are getting womanly and cowardly."

I warned him that there was danger ahead, and that, with his permission, as I had a depot of goods in the nation, I would watch them a while longer. We then packed up and publicly left the ground, and rode twelve miles to the Big Spring, where Colonel Hawkins agreed to halt for a day or two, and I returned at night to the vicinity of the council ground, where I fell in with young Bill Milfort, a handsome half-blood, nearly white, whom I had once nursed through a dangerous illness. Bill—alas! that he should have been doomed to perish by my hand —was strongly attached to me, and agreed to apprise me when Tecumseh was ready to deliver his talk.

Next day, precisely at twelve, Bill summoned me. I saw the Shawnees issue from their lodge; they were painted black, and entirely naked except the flap about their loins. Every weapon but the war-club—then first introduced among the Creeks—had been laid aside.

An angry scowl sat on all their visages: they looked like a procession of devils. Tecumseh led, the warriors followed, one in the footsteps of the other. The Creeks, in dense masses, stood on each side of the path, but the Shawnees noticed no one; they marched to the pole in the centre of the square, and then turned to the left.

At each angle of the square Tecumseh took from his pouch some tobacco and sumach, and dropped it on the ground; his warriors performed the same ceremony. This they repeated three times as they marched around the square. Then they approached the flag-pole in the centre, circled round it three times, and, facing the north, threw tobacco and sumach on a small fire, burning, as usual, near the base of the pole. On this they emptied their pouches.

They then marched in the same order to the council, or king's house (as it was termed in ancient times), and drew up before it. The Big Warrior and the leading men were sitting there.

The Shawnee chief sounded his war-whoop—a most diabolical yell—and each of his followers responded. Tecumseh then presented to the Big Warrior a wampum-belt of five different-colored strands, which the Creek chief handed to his warriors, and it was passed down the line.

The Shawnee pipe was then produced; it was large, long, and profusely decorated with shells, beads, and painted eagle and porcupine quills. It was lighted from the fire in the centre, and slowly passed from the Big Warrior along the line.

All this time not a word had been uttered; every thing was still as death: even the winds slept, and there was only the gentle rustle of the falling leaves.

At length Tecumseh spoke, at first slowly and in sonorous tones; but soon he grew impassioned, and the words fell in avalanches from his lips. His eyes burned with supernatural lustre, and his whole frame trembled with emotion: his voice resounded over the multitude—now sinking in low and musical whispers, now rising to its highest key, hurling out his words like a succession of thunderbolts.

His countenance varied with his speech: its prevalent expression was a sneer of hatred and defiance; sometimes a murderous smile; for a brief interval a sentiment of profound sorrow pervaded it; and, at the close, a look of concentrated vengeance, such, I suppose, as distinguishes the arch-enemy of mankind. I have heard many great orators, but I never saw one with the vocal powers of Tecumseh, or the same command of the muscles of his face.

Had I been deaf, the play of his countenance would have told me what he said. Its effect on that wild, superstitious, untutored, and warlike assemblage may be conceived: not a word was said, but stern warriors, the "stoics of the woods," shook with emotion, and a thousand tomahawks were brandished in the air.

Even the Big Warrior, who had been true to the whites, and remained faithful during the war, was, for the moment, visibly affected, and more than once I saw his huge hand clutch, spasmodically, the handle of his knife.

All this was the effect of his delivery; for, though the mother of Tecumseh was a Creek, and he was familiar with the language, he spoke in the northern dialect, and it was afterward interpreted by an Indian linguist to the assembly. His speech has been reported, but no one has done or can do it justice. I think I can repeat the substance of what he said, and, indeed, his very words.

TECUMSEH'S SPEECH

"In defiance of the white warriors of Ohio and Kentucky, I have traveled through their settlements, once our favorite hunting grounds. No war-

whoop was sounded, but there is blood on our knives. The Palefaces felt the blow, but knew not whence it came.

"Accursed be the race that has seized on our country and made women of our warriors. * Our fathers, from their tombs, reproach us as slaves and cowards. I hear them now in the wailing winds.

"The Muscogee was once a mighty people. The Georgians trembled at your warwhoop, and the maidens of my tribe, on the distant lakes, sung the prowess of your warriors and sighed for their embraces.

"Now your very blood is white; your tomahawks have no edge; your bows and arrows were buried with your fathers. Oh!

Muscogees, brethren of my mother, brush from your eyelids the sleep of slavery; once more strike for vengeance—once more for your country. The spirits of the mighty dead complain. Their tears drop from the weeping skies. Let the white race perish.

"They seize your land; they corrupt your women; they trample on the ashes of your dead!

"Back, whence they came, upon a trail of blood, they must be driven.

"Back! back, ay, into the great water whose accursed waves brought them to our shores!

"Burn their dwellings! Destroy their stock! Slay their wives and children! The Red Man owns the country, and the Palefaces must never enjoy it.

"War now! War forever! War upon the living! War upon the dead! Dig their very corpses from the grave. Our country must give no rest to a white man's bones.

"This is the will of the Great Spirit, revealed to my brother, his familiar, the Prophet of the Lakes. He sends me to you.

"All the tribes of the north are dancing the war-dance. Two mighty warriors across the seas will send us arms.

"Tecumseh will soon return to his country. My prophets shall tarry with you. They will stand between you and the bullets of your enemies. When the white men approach you the yawning earth shall swallow them up.

"Soon shall you see my arm of fire stretched athwart the sky. I will stamp my foot at Tippecanoe, and the very earth shall shake."*

When he resumed his seat the northern pipe was again passed round in solemn silence. The Shawnees then simultaneously leaped up with one appalling yell, and danced their tribal war-dance, going through the evolutions of battle, the scout, the ambush, the final struggle, brandishing their war-clubs, and screaming in terrific concert an infernal harmony fit only for the regions of the damned.

It was now midnight, and I left the ground and made the best of my way to Colonel Hawkins's camp at Big Spring, reporting faithfully to him what had occurred; but he appeared to attach little importance to it, relying too much on his own influence over the Indians.

"Colonel Hawkins," says Pickett, in his "*History of Alabama*," "seems to have been strangely benighted, slowly allowing his mind to be convinced that any thing serious was meditated."

He had resided many years among the Creeks, and early conceived the laudable notion of teaching them the arts of civilization. In his communications to the War Department he flattered himself that they emulated the progress of the whites, and that the whole nation, with the exception of a few "fanatics" without influence, sincerely desired peace.

Even after the Creeks and Shawnees had visited Pensacola to procure ammunition, and informed Forbes and Inerarity that they meant to attack the Tensaw settlements, Colonel Hawkins assured General Flournoy that there was no danger.

He over-estimated his own influence, and I ventured to tell him so as we rode from Big Spring. It was under this unfortunate advice, it will be seen, that General Flournoy subsequently refused General Claiborne's urgent application for orders to march into the heart of the Creek nation, and directed him to remain on the defensive and turn his attention chiefly "to the security of Mobile."

The correspondence of General Wilkinson, General Flournoy, Judge Toulmin, Colonel George S. Gaines, Colonel John M'Kee, and all the leading men on the frontier, refer to this opinion of Colonel Hawkins.

He believed that it would be a mere civil war for power among the chiefs and tribal factions, and that he would be able to restrain them. He continued to cherish this opinion until menaced with danger that compelled him to remove his family into Georgia and withdraw from his post.

He was an old and faithful officer—a man of fine sense—a sterling patriot, and of cool and unflinching courage. He loved the Indians; they had great confidence in him; but he was, unhappily, deceived on this occasion.

At the battle of the Holy Ground, which occurred some time after, the prophets left by Tecumseh predicted that the earth would yawn and swallow up General Claiborne and his troops. Tecumseh refers to the Kings of England and Spain, who supplied the Indians with arms at Detroit and at Pensacola. The British officers had informed him that a comet would soon appear, and the earthquakes of 1811 had commenced as he came through Kentucky. Like a consummate orator, he refers to them in his speech. When the comet soon after appeared, and the earth began to tremble, they attributed to him supernatural powers, and immediately took up arms.

BIBLIOGRAPHY

1. Brooks, Robert Preston, Atkinson, Mentzer; *History of Georgia, 1913 - Georgia*

2. Monette, John Wesley, *History of the Discovery and Settlement of the Valley of the Mississippi, by the Three Great European Powers, Spain, France, and Great Britain: And the Subsequent Occupation, Settlement and Extension of Civil Government by the United States Until the Year 1846, Volume 2*, Harper & Brothers, 1846

3. Hamilton, Peter J., *Publications of the Alabama Historical Society: Miscellaneous Collections* By Alabama Historical Society, 1901

4. Taylor, Thomas Jones, *EARLY HISTORY OF MADISON COUNTY And, Incidentally of North Alabama,* Chapter IV – Settlement by Pioneers 1805 to 1809

5. Brewer, George Evans, *History of Coosa County,* The Alabama Historical Quarterly, Vol. 04, No. 01, Spring Issue 1942, Chapter one

6. Ball, T. H., *A glance into The Great South-East, or, Clarke County, Alabama, and it's surroundings, from 1540 to 1877*

7. Claiborne, John Francis Hamtramck, Life and Times of Gen. Sam Dale: The Mississippi Partisan, Harper & Brothers, 1860

8. Pickett, Albert James HISTORY OF ALABAMA and incidentally of MISSISSIPPI and GEORGIA, 1896

9. Saunders, Col James Edmonds EARLY SETTLERS OF ALABAMA Notes and Genealogies, 1899

10. Brewer, W *ALABAMA HER HISTORY WAR RECORD and PUBLIC MEN,* 1872

11. Record, James *A DREAM COME TRUE The Story of Madison County and incidentally of Alabama and the United States*

12. Publications of the Alabama Historical Society: Miscellaneous Collections *By Alabama Historical Society*

13. Riley, Rev. B. J. *History of Conecuh County,* 1881

Dear Reader,

As an author, I love feedback. I enjoy sharing stories about Alabama's history on www.alabamapioneers.com.

I need to ask a favor. Reviews can be tough to come by these days. You, the reader, have the power to make or break a book. If you're so inclined, I'd greatly appreciate a review or simply a comment about *Alabama Footprints - Settlement* or on any of my books on Amazon.com or Barnes and Noble. I read each one and take them to heart when I write.

While you are online, you might want to check out my other *Alabama Footprints* books, as well as my historical fiction series, *Tapestry of Love*, which was inspired by the true story and events of the Cottingham family who settled on the Eastern Shore of Virginia and imigrated to Alabama in the early 1800s. You can see all my books and contact me through my Amazon Author page link below:
http://www.amazon.com/Donna-R-Causey/e/B0052HE4S0/

or my facebook pages:

www.facebook.com/alabamapioneers

www.facebook.com/daysgonebyme

http://www.facebook.com/ribbonoflove

In gratitude,
Donna R. Causey

Read more books of the The Alabama Footprints Series

**ALABAMA FOOTPRINTS
Exploration**

**ALABAMA FOOTPRINTS
Settlement**

**ALABAMA FOOTPRINTS
Pioneers**

More coming soon!

Additional information on Alabama can be found on the websites:

www.alabamapioneers.com

www.daysgoneby.me

Follow on Facebook at:

www.facebook.com/alabamapioneers

www.facebook.com/daysgonebyme

http://www.facebook.com/ribbonoflove

and

Twitter

http://twitter.com/alabamapioneers

Other nonfiction and fictional books by Donna R. Causey can be found
at
Barnes and Noble
or
Amazon.com

Follow Donna R. Causey on

www.facebook.com/alabamapioneers

www.facebook.com/daysgonebyme

http://www.facebook.com/ribbonoflove

or on

Donna R. Causey's websites

www.alabamapioneers.com

www.daysgoneby.me

Made in the USA
Lexington, KY
26 November 2015